Knative Cookbook

*Building Effective Serverless Applications
with Kubernetes and OpenShift*

Burr Sutter and Kamesh Sampath

Beijing · Boston · Farnham · Sebastopol · Tokyo

Knative Cookbook

by Burr Sutter and Kamesh Sampath

Copyright © 2020 Red Hat, Inc. All rights reserved.

Published by O'Reilly Media, Inc., 1005 Gravenstein Highway North, Sebastopol, CA 95472.

O'Reilly books may be purchased for educational, business, or sales promotional use. Online editions are also available for most titles (*http://oreilly.com*). For more information, contact our corporate/institutional sales department: 800-998-9938 or *corporate@oreilly.com*.

Acquisitions Editor: John Devins	**Indexer:** Potomac Indexing, LLC
Development Editor: Jeff Bleiel	**Interior Designer:** David Futato
Production Editor: Christopher Faucher	**Cover Designer:** Karen Montgomery
Copyeditor: Kim Cofer	**Illustrator:** Rebecca Demarest
Proofreader: Tom Sullivan	

April 2020:   First Edition

Revision History for the First Edition
2020-04-01:   First Release
2020-11-13:   Second Release

See *http://oreilly.com/catalog/errata.csp?isbn=9781492061199* for release details.

The O'Reilly logo is a registered trademark of O'Reilly Media, Inc. *Knative Cookbook*, the cover image, and related trade dress are trademarks of O'Reilly Media, Inc.

The views expressed in this work are those of the authors, and do not represent the publisher's views. While the publisher and the authors have used good faith efforts to ensure that the information and instructions contained in this work are accurate, the publisher and the authors disclaim all responsibility for errors or omissions, including without limitation responsibility for damages resulting from the use of or reliance on this work. Use of the information and instructions contained in this work is at your own risk. If any code samples or other technology this work contains or describes is subject to open source licenses or the intellectual property rights of others, it is your responsibility to ensure that your use thereof complies with such licenses and/or rights.

This work is part of a collaboration between O'Reilly and Red Hat, Inc. See our *statement of editorial independence* (*https://oreil.ly/editorial-independence*).

978-1-492-06119-9

[LSI]

Table of Contents

Preface

Serverless architecture has recently taken center stage in cloud native application deployment. Enterprises started to see the benefits that serverless applications bring to them, such as agility, rapid deployment, and resource cost optimization. As with any other new technology, there were multiple ways to approach and/or employ serverless technologies, such as Function as a Service (FaaS) and Backend as a Service (BaaS)—that is, running your applications as ephemeral containers—with the ability to scale up and down.

Knative (*https://knative.dev*) was started with the simple goal of having a Kubernetes-native platform to build, deploy, and manage your serverless workloads. Kubernetes solves a lot of cloud native application problems, but with a fair bit of complexity, especially from the perspective of deployment. To make a simple service deployment with Kubernetes, a developer has to write a minimum of two YAMLs (*https:// yaml.org*), such as a Deployment service, and then perform the necessary plumbing work to expose the service to the outside world. The complexity makes an application developer spend more time crafting the YAMLs and other core platform tasks rather than focusing on the business need.

Knative tries to solve these Kubernetes problems by providing all essential middleware primitives via a simpler deployment model. On Knative you can deploy any modern application workload, such as monolithic applications, microservices, or even tiny functions. Knative can run in any cloud platform that runs Kubernetes, which gives enterprises more agility and flexibility in running their serverless workloads without relying on cloud vendor–specific features.

Why We Wrote This Book

The fact there are "many" ways to do serverless has resulted in confusion among developers, with following questions being raised immediately:

1. What implementation should I choose: FaaS or BaaS?
2. What is the quickest way to get started?
3. What are the use cases for which I can apply serverless technology?
4. How do I measure the benefits?
5. What tools I should use to develop the serverless applications?

We had the same set of questions when we started to explore serverless technology. The problems and challenges that we faced during our research became the crux of this cookbook. This book serves as a practical guide in how to solve those challenges, with detailed examples.

It is called a "cookbook" because the examples are structured as "recipes," each with a Problem, Solution, and a Discussion with possible detailed explanations. As it is impossible to cover all possible serverless methods listed earlier, we decided to choose BaaS. Knative is a Kubernetes-based platform that helps to run your serverless workload in the BaaS way.

Who Should Read This Book

This book is for for architects and developers who have a solid understanding of Kubernetes core concepts and who wish to enhance their knowledge in building real-world applications with Knative.

Conventions Used in This Book

The following typographical conventions are used in this book:

Italic
    Indicates new terms, URLs, email addresses, filenames, and file extensions.

`Constant width`
    Used for program listings, as well as within paragraphs to refer to program elements such as variable or function names, databases, data types, environment variables, statements, and keywords.

`Constant width bold`
    Shows commands or other text that should be typed literally by the user.

Constant width italic

Shows text that should be replaced with user-supplied values or by values deter-mined by context.

This element signifies a tip or suggestion.

This element signifies a general note.

This element indicates a warning or caution.

Using Code Examples

You can download this book's source code from our GitHub Repo (*https://github.com/ redhat-developer-demos/knative-tutorial/tree/knative-cookbook*) as a ZIP file or clone the repository locally using git, as shown here:

```
$ git clone -b knative-cookbook
https://github.com/redhat-developer-demos/knative-tutorial
```

$BOOK_HOME is a variable that refers to the source code directory on your machine where you downloaded the recipe code examples.

If you have a technical question or a problem using the code examples, please send email to *bookquestions@oreilly.com*.

This book is here to help you get your job done. In general, if example code is offered with this book, you may use it in your programs and documentation. You do not need to contact us for permission unless you're reproducing a significant portion of the code. For example, writing a program that uses several chunks of code from this book does not require permission. Selling or distributing examples from O'Reilly books does require permission. Answering a question by citing this book and quoting example code does not require permission. Incorporating a significant amount of example code from this book into your product's documentation does require permission.

We appreciate, but generally do not require, attribution. An attribution usually includes the title, author, publisher, and ISBN. For example: "*Knative Cookbook* by Burr Sutter and Kamesh Sampath (O'Reilly). Copyright 2020 O'Reilly Media Inc., 978-1-492-06119-9."

If you feel your use of code examples falls outside fair use or the permission given above, feel free to contact us at *permissions@oreilly.com*.

Staying Up to Date

Though we try to stay with latest version of Knative for this book, Knative is evolving at a rapid rate. To keep up with the latest developments, we suggest that you keep an eye on the upstream community project page (*http://knative.dev*) as well as Red Hat's evolving Knative Tutorial (*https://redhat-developer-demos.github.io/knative-tutorial*).

O'Reilly Online Learning

 For more than 40 years, *O'Reilly Media* has provided technology and business training, knowledge, and insight to help companies succeed.

Our unique network of experts and innovators share their knowledge and expertise through books, articles, and our online learning platform. O'Reilly's online learning platform gives you on-demand access to live training courses, in-depth learning paths, interactive coding environments, and a vast collection of text and video from O'Reilly and 200+ other publishers. For more information, please visit *http://oreilly.com*.

How to Contact Us

Please address comments and questions concerning this book to the publisher:

O'Reilly Media, Inc.
1005 Gravenstein Highway North
Sebastopol, CA 95472
800-998-9938 (in the United States or Canada)
707-829-0515 (international or local)
707-829-0104 (fax)

We have a web page for this book, where we list errata, examples, and any additional information. You can access this page at *https://oreil.ly/knative-cookbook*.

Email *bookquestions@oreilly.com* to comment or ask technical questions about this book.

For more information about our books, courses, and news, see our website at *http://www.oreilly.com*.

Find us on Facebook: *http://facebook.com/oreilly*

Follow us on Twitter: *http://twitter.com/oreillymedia*

Watch us on YouTube: *http://www.youtube.com/oreillymedia*

Acknowledgments

Reviewers

Many thanks to our reviewers! They all provided valuable feedback, suggestions, and in some cases alternate solutions; pointed out issues we had overlooked; and in general greatly improved the book. Any errors or omissions in this text are ours and not theirs. An excellent example of their wisdom is the correct observation, "That sentence doesn't know whether it's coming or going!"

First Edition: Roland Huss, Matthias Wessendorf, Nicola Ferraro, and Vincent Demeester. Special note of thanks to Ben Browning, Markus Thömmes, and William Markito from the Red Hat Engineering team.

O'Reilly

Thanks to the entire team at O'Reilly, without whom this book would not exist for many reasons, and if it did the content wouldn't be or look nearly as good!

First Edition: our editors Jeff Bleiel and Sarah Grey.

From the Authors

Burr Sutter

My thanks go first and foremost to Kamesh Sampath—who performed the lion's share of the work required to create this book—for his expansive technical knowledge and insight, and his relentless diligence and determination in researching, debugging, using, and documenting new technologies like Knative so they become more accessible to the developer community at large.

I am also grateful to the unimaginably diverse global developer community I engage with every day, many of whom have made profound sacrifices to access knowledge and opportunity. There is no question that these are—and will continue to be—the true digital heroes, influencers, change agents, kingmakers, and re-definers of our future. Their efforts remind me that greatness and future impact will be determined not only by talent, but also by an unflinching determination and hunger to learn and imagine and create and master. The opportunity I have as a developer advocate to contribute to these shapers of the future is one of my greatest privileges.

Kamesh Sampath

Thanks to my mentor, manager, and coauthor Burr Sutter for working on this project. His experience and guidance not only helped getting this book into shape, but also allowed me to learn from many different perspectives.

Thanks to Red Hat and Red Hat Developers for giving me this opportunity to author my very first book.

Thanks to my wife who has been a great support to me and without whom I would not have written this book. I should take this moment to thank my son, who does not understand what I am writing but his curious questions like, "Dad, where are you with your book?" or "How is the book coming up?" kept fueling my energy to go that extra mile :).

Thanks all my Gods and Gurus; without their blessings nothing would have been possible.

Last but not least, I wish to extend my gratitude and thanks to all developers who read this book. Without you, the "Developer Community," we would have never thought to write this book.

CHAPTER 1

Getting Started with Knative

Deploying applications as serverless services is becoming a popular architectural style. It seems like many organizations assume that *Function as a Service (FaaS)* is serverless. We think it is more accurate to say that FaaS is one way to do serverless, but not the only way. This raises a super critical question for enterprises that may have applications which could be a monolith or a microservice: What is the easiest path to serverless application deployment?

The answer is a platform that can run serverless workloads, while enabling you to have complete control over how to configure, build, deploy, and run applications—ideally, a platform that would support deploying the applications as Linux containers. In this chapter we introduce you to one such platform—Knative—that helps you to run the serverless workloads in a Kubernetes-native way.

A Kubernetes cluster does not come with Knative and its dependencies pre-installed, so the recipes in this chapter detail how to have Knative and its dependencies installed into a Kubernetes cluster. The recipes also help in setting up your local developer environment that will be required to run the exercises in this book.

1.1 Installing the Required Tools

Problem

You want to equip your local developer environment with the tools you will need to build, deploy, and run Kubernetes-based applications.

Solution

In general, you will need several of the open source tools listed in Table 1-1.

Table 1-1. CLI tools

Tool	macOS	Fedora	Windows
`git`	Download (*https://oreil.ly/ wHGBs*)	Download (*https://oreil.ly/ TV0qp*)	Download (*https://oreil.ly/ miQPZ*)
`docker`	Docker for Mac (*https:// oreil.ly/ryFI0*)	`dnf install docker`	Docker for Windows (*https:// oreil.ly/cctEu*)
kubectl (*https://oreil.ly/RLPVR*)	Download (*https://oreil.ly/ TMzIC*)	Download (*https://oreil.ly/ BUM6G*)	Download (*https://oreil.ly/ 8E7zA*)
helm (*https://helm.sh*)	Install (*https://helm.sh/ docs/intro/install*)	Install (*https://helm.sh/ docs/intro/install*)	Install (*https://helm.sh/docs/ intro/install*)
stern (*https://oreil.ly/XjESP*)	`brew install stern`	Download (*https:// oreil.ly/-nTTz*)	Download (*https://oreil.ly/ ALPob*)
yq v2.4.1 (*https://oreil.ly/i4Q15*)	Download (*https://oreil.ly/ hMUqW*)	Download (*https://oreil.ly/ K4nue*)	Download (*https://oreil.ly/7- YcH*)
httpie (*https://httpie.org*)	`brew install httpie`	`dnf install httpie`	Install (*https://httpie.org/ doc#windows-etc*)
hey (*https://github.com/rakyll/hey*)	Download (*https://oreil.ly/ e8pJc*)	Download (*https://oreil.ly/ f1OHE*)	Download (*https://oreil.ly/ j1T-h*)
watch	`brew install watch`	`dnf install procps-ng`	
kubectx and kubens	`brew install kubectx`	Install (*https://oreil.ly/ 38Vf_*)	

> Make sure you add all the tools to your $PATH before you proceed with any of the recipes in upcoming chapters.

Discussion

The following is a list of the tools you'll need with minimum and recommended versions:

> The versions listed here were the ones tested at the time this book was written. Later versions should maintain backward compatibility with the use cases used in this cookbook's recipes.

git

A distributed version-control system for tracking changes in source code during software development:

```
$ git version
git version 2.21.0
```

docker

A client to run the Linux containers:

```
$ docker --version
Docker version 19.03.5, build 633a0ea
```

kubectl

Knative minimum requires Kubernetes v1.15+; however, we recommend using v1.15.0. To check your kubectl version run:

```
$ kubectl version --short
Client Version: v1.15.0
Server Version: v1.15.0
```

helm

Helps you define, install, and upgrade even the most complex Kubernetes applications:

```
$ helm version
version.BuildInfo{Version:"v3.0.2"...}
```

stern

Allows you to tail multiple pods on Kubernetes and multiple containers within the pod:

```
$ stern --version
stern version 1.11.0
```

yq

A lightweight and portable command-line YAML processor:

```
$ yq --version
yq version 2.4.1
```

httpie

A command-line HTTP client that will make you smile:

```
$ http --version
1.0.3
```

hey

A tiny program that sends some load to a web application.

hey does not have a version option, so you can use hey --help to verify that it is in your *$PATH*.

watch

Execute a program periodically, showing output in full screen:

```
$ watch --version
watch from procps-ng 3.3.15
```

kubectx

Allows you to switch faster between clusters and namespaces.

kubectx does not have a version option, so you can use `kubectx --help` to verify that it is in your *$PATH*.

kubens is installed with kubectx, so you can use `kubens --help` to verify that it is in your *$PATH*.

1.2 Setting Up a Kubernetes Cluster

Problem

You want to set up a Kubernetes cluster in your local development environment.

Solution

You can use minikube (*https://oreil.ly/euHI1*) as your Kubernetes cluster for a local development environment. Minikube provides a single-node Kubernetes cluster that is best suited for local development. Download minikube and add it to your *$PATH*.

All the recipes in this book have been tested with minikube v1.7.2 and the Kubernetes CLI (kubectl) v1.15.0.

The script *$BOOK_HOME/bin/start-minikube.sh* helps you start minikube with the right configuration.

Discussion

You will also need to know the following list of environment variables and their default values:

PROFILE_NAME

The name of minikube profile; default is `knativecookbook`

MEMORY

The memory that will be allocated to the minikube virtual machine (VM); default is 8GB

CPUS

The number of CPUs that will be allocated to the minikube VM; default is 4

VM_DRIVER

The virtual machine driver that will be used:

- For macOS use `virtualbox`

- For Linux use `kmv2`

- For Windows use `hyper-v`

VM_DRIVER is a required environment variable and the *start-minikube.sh* script will fail to start if it is not set:

```
$ $BOOK_HOME/bin/start-minikube.sh
✕ profile "knativecookbook" not found
✅ Created a new profile : knativecookbook
✅ minikube profile was successfully set to knativecookbook
😄 [knativecookbook] minikube v1.6.2 on Darwin 10.15.2
✚ Selecting virtualbox driver from user configuration (alternates: [hyperkit])
🔥 Creating virtualbox VM (CPUs=4, Memory=8192MB, Disk=50000MB) ...
🐳 Preparing Kubernetes v1.15.0 on Docker 19.03.5 ...
    ▪ apiserver.enable-admission-plugins=LimitRanger,NamespaceExists,
      NamespaceLifecycle,ResourceQuota,ServiceAccount,DefaultStorageClass,
      MutatingAdmissionWebhook
🚜 Pulling images ...
🚀 Launching Kubernetes ...
⌛ Waiting for cluster to come online ...
🏄 Done! kubectl is now configured to use "knativecookbook"
```

1.3 Installing the Internal Kubernetes Container Registry

Problem

You need to push and pull container images into and from a container registry. To do that you will need to install the internal container registry first.

Solution

To set up an internal container registry inside of minikube, run:

```
$ minikube addons enable registry
```

It will take a few minutes for the registry to be enabled; you can watch the status of the pods on the kube-system namespace.

Discussion

If the registry enablement is successful, you will see two new pods in the kube-system namespace with a status of Running:

```
$ kubectl get pods -n kube-system
NAME                         READY   STATUS    RESTARTS   AGE
registry-7c5hg               1/1     Running   0          29m
```

```
registry-proxy-cj6dj          1/1    Running   0          29m
...
```

1.4 Configuring Container Registry Aliases

Problem

You want to use custom domain names to push and pull container images into an internal container registry.

Solution

As part of some recipes in this cookbook, you will need interact with the local internal registry. To make push and pull smoother, we have provided a helper script that enables you to use some common names like dev.local and example.com as registry aliases for the internal registry. Navigate to the registry helper folder and run:

```
$ cd $BOOK_HOME/apps/minikube-registry-helper
```

A daemonset (*https://oreil.ly/N-QS8*) is used to run the same copy of the pod in all the nodes of the Kubernetes cluster. Run the following command to deploy the registry helper daemonset and ConfigMap (*https://oreil.ly/mTp6X*) that will be used by the registry helper:

```
$ kubectl apply -n kube-system -f registry-aliases-config.yaml
$ kubectl apply -n kube-system -f node-etc-hosts-update.yaml
```

> Wait for the daemonset to be running before proceeding to the next step. You can monitor the status of the daemonset with watch kubectl get pods -n kube-system. You can use Ctrl-C to terminate the watch.

Verify that the entries are added to your minikube node's */etc/hosts* file:

```
watch minikube ssh -- sudo cat /etc/hosts
```

A successful daemonset execution will update the minikube node's */etc/hosts* file with the following entries:

```
127.0.0.1       localhost
127.0.1.1       demo
10.111.151.121  dev.local
10.111.151.121  example.com
```

The IP for dev.local and example.com will match the CLUSTER-IP of the internal container registry. To verify this, run:

```
$ kubectl get svc registry -n kube-system
NAME       TYPE       CLUSTER-IP      PORT(S)   AGE
registry   ClusterIP  10.111.151.121  80/TCP    178m
```

As part of the last step of configuring the internal container registry, you also need to patch the CoreDNS so that the deployments resolve container images that have names that begin with dev.local and example.com (e.g., dev.local/rhdevelopers/foo:v1.0.0):

```
$ ./patch-coredns.sh
```

To verify that the patch was successfully executed, run the following command to get the contents of the coredns ConfigMap in the kube-system namespace:

```
$ kubectl get cm -n kube-system coredns -o yaml
```

A successfully patched coredns ConfigMap will have the following content:

```
apiVersion: v1
data:
  Corefile: |-
    .:53 {
        errors
        health
        rewrite name dev.local registry.kube-system.svc.cluster.local ❶
        rewrite name example.com registry.kube-system.svc.cluster.local
        kubernetes cluster.local in-addr.arpa ip6.arpa {
            pods insecure
            upstream
            fallthrough in-addr.arpa ip6.arpa
        }
        prometheus :9153
        proxy . /etc/resolv.conf
        cache 30
        loop
        reload
        loadbalance
    }
kind: ConfigMap
metadata:
  name: coredns
```

❶ The rewrite rule will resolve dev.local to the internal registry address registry.kube-system.svc.cluster.local.

Discussion

You may need to update the custom domain names for the internal container registry. In order update it, you need to edit the ConfigMap *registry-aliases-config.yaml* and add the extra domain names as per your needs. Each domain name should be on a new line of its own. For example, the following snippet shows how to add a new domain called `test.org` to the registry helper ConfigMap:

```
apiVersion: v1
data:
  # Add additional hosts separated by new-line
  registryAliases: >-
    dev.local
    example.com
    test.org
  # default registry address in minikube when enabled
  # via minikube addons enable registry
  registrySvc: registry.kube-system.svc.cluster.local
kind: ConfigMap
metadata:
  name: registry-aliases
  namespace: kube-system
```

After you update the ConfigMap, you need to restart the daemonset by deleting the daemonset pod in the `kube-system` namespace. When the daemonset restarts, it will pick up new aliases from the registry helper ConfigMap and configure the same to be used as domain aliases. After a successful restart of the daemonset, you need to rerun the script *patch-coredns.sh* to patch the CoreDNS.

1.5 Installing Istio

Problem

You need to install an ingress gateway in order to interact with Knative Services.

Solution

Knative Serving requires an ingress gateway to route requests to the Knative Serving Services. Currently it supports the following ingress gateways that are based on Envoy:

- Ambassador (*https://www.getambassador.io*)
- Contour (*https://projectcontour.io*)
- Gloo (*https://docs.solo.io/gloo/latest*)
- Istio (*https://istio.io*)

In this recipe we will use Istio. Since the ingress gateway is the only Istio component required for Knative, you can set up a minimal Istio (istio lean) installation with the following script:

```
$ $BOOK_HOME/bin/install-istio.sh
```

Discussion

Installing Istio components will take some time, so we highly recommend that you start the Knative components installation only *after* you have verified that the Istio component pods are running. The install script will terminate automatically after all the needed Istio components and Custom Resource Definitions (CRDs) have been installed and running.

All Istio resources will be under one of the following application programming interface (API) groups:

- authentication.istio.io
- config.istio.io
- networking.istio.io
- rbac.istio.io

You can verify that the needed CRDs are available by querying `api-resources` for each API group:

```
$ kubectl api-resources --api-group=networking.istio.io
NAME                APIGROUP               NAMESPACED   KIND
destinationrules    networking.istio.io    true         DestinationRule
envoyfilters        networking.istio.io    true         EnvoyFilter
gateways            networking.istio.io    true         Gateway
serviceentries      networking.istio.io    true         ServiceEntry
sidecars            networking.istio.io    true         Sidecar
virtualservices     networking.istio.io    true         VirtualService

$ kubectl api-resources --api-group=config.istio.io
NAME                APIGROUP               NAMESPACED   KIND
adapters            config.istio.io        true         adapter
attributemanifests  config.istio.io        true         attributemanifest
handlers            config.istio.io        true         handler
httpapispecbindings config.istio.io        true         HTTPAPISpecBinding
httpapispecs        config.istio.io        true         HTTPAPISpec
instances           config.istio.io        true         instance
quotaspecbindings   config.istio.io        true         QuotaSpecBinding
quotaspecs          config.istio.io        true         QuotaSpec
rules               config.istio.io        true         rule
templates           config.istio.io        true         template

$ kubectl api-resources --api-group=authentication.istio.io
NAME                APIGROUP                       NAMESPACED   KIND
```

```
meshpolicies          authentication.istio.io  false    MeshPolicy
policies              authentication.istio.io  true     Policy

$ kubectl api-resources --api-group=rbac.istio.io
NAME                     APIGROUP         NAMESPACED  KIND
authorizationpolicies    rbac.istio.io    true        AuthorizationPolicy
clusterrbacconfigs       rbac.istio.io    false       ClusterRbacConfig
rbacconfigs              rbac.istio.io    true        RbacConfig
servicerolebindings      rbac.istio.io    true        ServiceRoleBinding
serviceroles             rbac.istio.io    true        ServiceRole
```

1.6 Installing Knative

Knative has two building blocks:

Knative Serving

Serving is for running your services inside Kubernetes by providing a simplified deployment syntax, with automated scale-to-zero and scale-out based on HTTP load.

Knative Eventing

Eventing is used to connect your Knative Serving Services to event streams beyond HTTP (e.g., an Apache Kafka topic).

The Knative installation process is divided into three steps:

1. Installing Knative Custom Resource Definitions (CRDs) (*https://oreil.ly/jsO1V*)
2. Installing the Knative Serving components
3. Installing the Knative Eventing components

This recipe shows how to install these components in the order listed here.

Problem

You need to install Knative CRDs, Knative Serving, and Knative Eventing components.

Solution

Knative Serving and Eventing define their own Kubernetes CRDs. You need to have the Knative Serving and Eventing CRDs installed in your Kubernetes cluster. Run the following command to do so:

```
$ kubectl apply --selector knative.dev/crd-install=true \
   --filename "https://github.com/knative/serving/releases/\
download/v0.12.0/serving.yaml" \
   --filename "https://github.com/knative/eventing/releases/\
download/v0.12.0/eventing.yaml"
```

Discussion

Now that you have installed the Knative Serving and Eventing CRDs, you can verify the CRDs by querying the `api-resources`, as described next.

All Knative Serving resources will be under the API group called `serving.knative.dev`:

```
$ kubectl api-resources --api-group=serving.knative.dev
NAME            SHORTNAMES      APIGROUP             NAMESPACED   KIND
configurations  config,cfg      serving.knative.dev  true         Configuration
revisions       rev             serving.knative.dev  true         Revision
routes          rt              serving.knative.dev  true         Route
services        kservice,ksvc   serving.knative.dev  true         Service
```

All Knative Eventing resources will be under one of the following API groups:

- `messaging.knative.dev`

- `eventing.knative.dev`

- `sources.eventing.knative.dev`

- `sources.knative.dev`

```
$ kubectl api-resources --api-group=messaging.knative.dev
NAME              SHORTNAMES   APIGROUP               NAMESPACED   KIND
channels          ch           messaging.knative.dev  true         Channel
inmemorychannels  imc          messaging.knative.dev  true         InMemoryChannel
parallels                      messaging.knative.dev  true         Parallel
sequences                      messaging.knative.dev  true         Sequence
subscriptions     sub          messaging.knative.dev  true         Subscription

$ kubectl api-resources --api-group=eventing.knative.dev
NAME         SHORTNAMES   APIGROUP              NAMESPACED   KIND
brokers                   eventing.knative.dev  true         Broker
eventtypes                eventing.knative.dev  true         EventType
triggers                  eventing.knative.dev  true         Trigger

$ kubectl api-resources --api-group=sources.eventing.knative.dev
NAME              APIGROUP                      NAMESPACED   KIND
apiserversources  sources.eventing.knative.dev  true         ApiServerSource
containersources  sources.eventing.knative.dev  true         ContainerSource
cronjobsources    sources.eventing.knative.dev  true         CronJobSource
sinkbindings      sources.eventing.knative.dev  true         SinkBinding

$ kubectl api-resources --api-group=sources.knative.dev
NAME              APIGROUP             NAMESPACED   KIND
apiserversources  sources.knative.dev  true         ApiServerSource
sinkbindings      sources.knative.dev  true         SinkBinding
```

Knative has two main infrastructure components: controller (*https://oreil.ly/OId3l*) and webhook (*https://oreil.ly/Cca0r*). These help in translating the Knative CRDs, which are usually written in YAML files, into Kubernetes objects like Deployment and Service. Apart from the controller and webhook, Knative Serving and Eventing also install their respective functional components, which are listed in the upcoming sections.

Run the following command to deploy the Knative Serving infrastructure components:

```
$ kubectl apply \
  --selector \
  networking.knative.dev/certificate-provider!=cert-manager \
  --filename \
  https://github.com/knative/serving/releases/download/v0.12.0/serving.yaml
```

This process will take a few minutes for the Knative Serving pods to be up and running. You can monitor the status of the Knative Serving installation by watching the pods in the knative-serving namespace using the command:

```
$ watch kubectl get pods -n knative-serving
NAME                              READY  STATUS   RESTARTS  AGE
activator-5dd6dc95bc-k9lg9        1/1    Running  0         86s
autoscaler-b56799cdf-55h5k        1/1    Running  0         86s
autoscaler-hpa-6f5c5cf986-b8lvg   1/1    Running  0         86s
controller-f8b98d964-qjxff        1/1    Running  0         85s
networking-istio-bb44d8c87-s2lbg  1/1    Running  0         85s
webhook-78dcbf4d94-dczd6          1/1    Running  0         85s
```

Run the following command to install Knative Eventing infrastructure components:

```
$ kubectl apply \
  --selector \
  networking.knative.dev/certificate-provider!=cert-manager \
  --filename \
  https://github.com/knative/eventing/releases/download/v0.12.0/eventing.yaml
```

Like the Knative Serving deployment, the Knative Eventing deployment will also take a few minutes to complete. You can watch the knative-eventing namespace pods for live status using the command:

```
$ watch kubectl get pods -n knative-eventing
NAME                                            READY  STATUS   RESTARTS  AGE
eventing-controller-77b4f76d56-d4fzf            1/1    Running  0         2m39s
eventing-webhook-f5d57b487-hbgps                1/1    Running  0         2m39s
imc-controller-65bb5ddf-kld5l                   1/1    Running  0         2m39s
imc-dispatcher-dd84879d7-qt2qn                  1/1    Running  0         2m39s
in-memory-channel-controller-6f74d5c8c8-vm44b   1/1    Running  0         2m39s
in-memory-channel-dispatcher-8db675949-mqmfk    1/1    Running  0         2m39s
sources-controller-79c4bf8b86-lxbjf             1/1    Running  0         2m39s
```

1.7 Verifying the Container Environment

Problem

You want to know that you have set the right minikube profile and are executing the commands in the right Docker context.

Solution

Minikube provides the `profile` and `docker-env` commands that are used to set the profile and configure your docker environment to use minikube. Run the following command to set your profile and docker environment for this book:

```
$ minikube profile knativecookbook
$ eval $(minikube docker-env)
```

Discussion

Now when you execute the command, `docker images` will list the images found inside of minikube's internal docker daemon (output shortened for brevity):

```
$ docker images --format {{.Repository}}
gcr.io/knative-releases/knative.dev/serving/cmd/activator
gcr.io/knative-releases/knative.dev/serving/cmd/webhook
gcr.io/knative-releases/knative.dev/serving/cmd/controller
gcr.io/knative-releases/knative.dev/serving/cmd/autoscaler-hpa
gcr.io/knative-releases/knative.dev/serving/cmd/networking/istio
k8s.gcr.io/kube-addon-manager
istio/proxyv2
istio/pilot
```

Creating Kubernetes Namespaces for This Book's Recipes

The recipes in each chapter will be deployed in the namespace dedicated for the chapter. Each chapter will instruct you to switch to the respective namespace. Run the following command to create all the required namespaces for this book:

```
$ kubectl create namespace chapter-2
$ kubectl create namespace chapter-3
$ kubectl create namespace chapter-4
$ kubectl create namespace chapter-5
$ kubectl create namespace chapter-6
$ kubectl create namespace chapter-7
```

Why Switch Namespaces?

Kubernetes by default creates the `default` namespace. You can control the namespace of the resource by specifying the `--namespace` or `-n` option to all your Kubernetes commands. By switching to the right namespace, you can be assured that your Kubernetes resources are created in the correct place as needed by the recipes.

You can use kubectl to switch to the required namespace. The following command shows how to use kubectl to switch to a namespace called chapter-1:

```
$ kubectl config set-context --current --namespace=chapter-1
```

Or you can use the kubens utility to set your current namespace to be chapter-1:

```
$ kubens chapter-1
```

 Setting your current namespace with kubens means you can avoid the option --namespace or its short name -n for all subsequent kubectl commands.

However, it is recommended that you continue to use --namespace or -n as part of your kubectl commands; using the namespace option ensures that you are creating Kubernetes resources in the correct namespace.

Ensure that you are also in the right working directory in your terminal by running the command:

```
$ cd $BOOK_HOME
```

Querying Kubernetes Resources

As part of the recipes, and many other places in the book, you will be instructed to watch Kubernetes resources.

You might be familiar with using the command kubectl get <resource> -w. You are free to use the kubectl command with the w option, but in this book we prefer to use the watch command. The watch command provides a simple and clean output that can help you to grok the output better. Let me explain the two variants with an example.

Let's assume you want to query running pods in a namespace called istio-system:

```
$ kubectl -n istio-system get pods -w
NAME                                          READY  STATUS            RESTARTS  AGE
cluster-local-gateway-7588cdfbc7-8f5s8        0/1    ContainerCreating 0         3s
istio-ingressgateway-5c87b8d6c7-dzwx8         0/1    ContainerCreating 0         4s
istio-pilot-7c555cf995-j9tpv                  0/1    ContainerCreating 0         4s
NAME                                          READY  STATUS            RESTARTS  AGE
istio-pilot-7c555cf995-j9tpv                  0/1    Running           0         16s
istio-ingressgateway-5c87b8d6c7-dzwx8         0/1    Running           0         27s
cluster-local-gateway-7588cdfbc7-8f5s8        0/1    Running           0         29s
istio-pilot-7c555cf995-j9tpv                  1/1    Running           0         36s
```

```
cluster-local-gateway-7588cdfbc7-8f5s8    1/1    Running           0          37s
istio-ingressgateway-5c87b8d6c7-dzwx8     1/1    Running           0          44s

$ watch kubectl -n istio-system get pods
NAME                                      READY  STATUS            RESTARTS   AGE
cluster-local-gateway-7588cdfbc7-vgwgw    1/1    Running           0          8s
istio-ingressgateway-5c87b8d6c7-tbj6g     1/1    Running           0          8s
istio-pilot-7c555cf995-6ggvv              1/1    Running           0          8s
```

If you compare the output of these two commands, you'll see that watch kubectl -n istio-system get pods has simple and clean output compared to kubectl -n istio-system get pods -w, although both command shows the same output. When using watch, the command kubectl -n istio-system get pods is refreshed every two seconds, which allows you to watch the changing status in a simpler way. By contrast, the kubectl watch option keeps appending to the output.

 In this book when you are instructed to watch some Kubernetes resource, you should use watch *<kubectl command>* as explained previously. However, the commands and options might vary from recipe to recipe.

You now have an understanding of what Knative is, how to install Knative and its dependencies, and how to install useful open source tools that will speed up your Kubernetes development.

With what you have learned in this chapter, you are all set to apply your Kubernetes knowledge to deploy serverless workloads. As part of the first step in putting your understanding to the test, Chapter 2 helps you by teaching you a few techniques on Knative Serving.

Understanding Knative Serving

Knative Serving is ideal for running your application services inside Kubernetes by providing a more simplified deployment syntax with automated scale-to-zero and scale-out based on HTTP load. The Knative platform will manage your service's deployments, revisions, networking, and scaling.

Knative Serving exposes your service via an HTTP URL and has a lot of safe defaults for its configurations. For many practical use cases you might need to tweak the defaults to your needs and might also need to adjust the traffic distribution among the service revisions. Because the Knative Serving Service has the built-in ability to automatically scale down to zero when not in use, it is appropriate to call it a *serverless service*.

In this chapter, we are going to deploy a Knative Serving Service, see its use of Configuration and Revision, and practice a blue-green deployment and Canary release.

Knative Serving Deployment Model

Before you deploy your first serverless service, it is important that you understand its deployment model and the Kubernetes resources that make up a Knative Service.

During the deployment of a Knative Serving Service (ksvc) as shown in Figure 2-1, the Knative Serving controller creates a Configuration, a Revision, and a Route, which deserve additional explanation:

Knative Configuration
> The *Knative Configuration* maintains the desired state of your deployment, providing a clean separation of code and configuration using the twelve-factor app development principles. Based on the desired state, the Knative Configuration controller creates a new Kubernetes Deployment for your application. Also, it's

important to note that every change to a Knative Configuration will result in a new Kubernetes Deployment.

Knative Revision

Since the Knative Configuration uses the twelve-factor app principles, every change to the application configuration creates a new *Knative Revision*. The Knative Revision is similar to a version control tag or label and it is immutable. Every Knative Revision has a corresponding Kubernetes Deployment associated with it; hence, it allows the application to be rolled back to any last known good configuration.

Knative Route

The *Knative Route* is the the URL by which the Knative Service can be accessed or invoked.

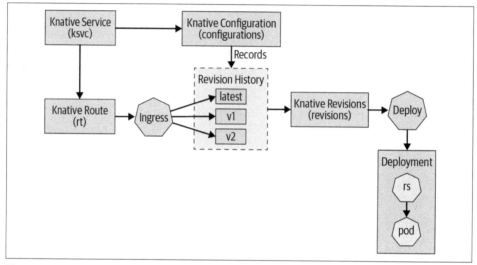

Figure 2-1. Knative Serving resources

 ksvc is the short name for the Knative Serving Service Custom Resource, and you can use the following command to query your Kubernetes cluster for this information:

```
kubectl api-resources --api-group=serving.knative.dev
```

Twelve-Factor App

12factor.net (*https://12factor.net*) defines the twelve-factor app as a methodology for building software-as-a-service apps that:

- Use declarative formats for setup automation, to minimize time and cost for new developers joining the project;
- Have a clean contract with the underlying operating system, offering maximum portability between execution environments;
- Are suitable for deployment on modern cloud platforms, obviating the need for servers and systems administration;
- Minimize divergence between development and production, enabling continuous deployment for maximum agility;
- And can scale up without significant changes to tooling, architecture, or development practices.

The twelve-factor methodology can be applied to apps written in any programming language, and which use any combination of backing services (database, queue, memory cache, etc.).

Before You Begin

All the recipes in this chapter will be executed from the directory *$BOOK_HOME/basics*, so change to the recipe directory by running:

```
$ cd $BOOK_HOME/basics
```

The recipes of this chapter will be deployed in the `chapter-2` namespace, so switch to the `chapter-2` namespace with the following command:

```
$ kubectl config set-context --current --namespace=chapter-2
```

2.1 Deploying a Knative Service

Problem

You want to deploy a microservice as a serverless service on Kubernetes.

Solution

Like any other Kubernetes resource, a Knative Serving Service can be deployed using a resource YAML file. As you will see, the resource YAML is similar to a Kubernetes Deployment but with a few attributes removed. For the upcoming recipes we will be using a prebuilt container image called quay.io/rhdevelopers/knative-tutorial-greeter:quarkus.

Before you deploy your first Knative Service, we need to quickly describe a Knative Service YAML:

```
apiVersion: serving.knative.dev/v1
kind: Service
metadata:
  name: greeter ❶
spec:
  template:
    metadata:
      name: greeter-v1 ❷
    spec:
      containers:
      - image: quay.io/rhdevelopers/knative-tutorial-greeter:quarkus
        livenessProbe:
          httpGet:
            path: /healthz
        readinessProbe:
          httpGet:
            path: /healthz
```

❶ The name of the service, in this case greeter, will become a prefix for all the generated Kubernetes resources that are created by this Knative Serving Service deployment.

❷ The name of the Knative Revision. If this name is not provided, Knative will create the revision name.

Run the following command to deploy the greeter Knative Service:

```
$ kubectl -n chapter-2 apply -f service.yaml
```

Discussion

As in any Kubernetes resource YAML, *apiVersion* defines the API group of the Knative Service. These API resources are available via the Kubernetes CRDs that you deployed as part of the setup described in Chapter 1. The *kind* is a Kubernetes Resource corresponding to the Knative Service. In order to avoid confusion with the Kubernetes built-in service, the Knative Service is associated with its apiVersion and kind—that is, service.serving.knative.dev.

The *spec* block of the resource YAML is exactly the same as the Kubernetes PodSpec (*https://oreil.ly/PUc_2*), with the following attributes removed:

- InitContainers
- RestartPolicy
- TerminationGracePeriodSeconds
- ActiveDeadlineSeconds
- DNSPolicy
- NodeSelector
- AutomountServiceAccountToken
- NodeName
- HostNetwork
- HostPID
- HostIPC
- ShareProcessNamespace
- SecurityContext
- Hostname
- Subdomain
- Affinity
- SchedulerName
- Tolerations
- HostAliases
- PriorityClassName
- Priority
- DNSConfig
- ReadinessGates
- RuntimeClassName

The block `spec → template` is called the Knative Service template block. The `meta data → name` in the service template defines the Knative Revision name. This name is optional and can be omitted; if it's omitted the Knative Revision name will be autogenerated.

The *liveness* probe of the Knative Service is slightly different from the standard Kubernetes probes (*https://oreil.ly/QdDXK*). It has no port defined as part of it probe definition; the Knative Serving controller can automatically infer the port and update it during the service deployment phase. The same rule is applicable for the *readiness* probe.

The very first deployment of the service will take additional time as the container image needs to be downloaded to your Kubernetes cluster. A successful deployment will result in a pod with a similar (though not identical) name in the `chapter-2` namespace:

```
$ watch kubectl get pods
NAME                                          READY   STATUS    AGE
greeter-v1-deployment-5749cc98fc-gs6zr        2/2     Running   10s
```

The deployment of a Knative Serving Service results in a `ksvc` being created. You can query for available `ksvc` services using the command `kubectl get ksvc`. In order to invoke the service you will need its URL, which is created by the Knative Route. To discover `greeter`'s Knative Route, run the following command:

```
$ kubectl -n chapter-2 get ksvc greeter
```

The preceding command will output the following (some columns omitted for brevity):

```
NAME       URL                                              LATESTCREATED   LATESTREADY
greeter    http://greeter.knativetutorial.example.com       greeter-v1      greeter-v1
```

The URL shown in the output is required to invoke the service. In your minikube environment you do not normally have a load balancer configured, therefore this URL has to be passed as a *Host* header by the calling client (e.g., `curl`). In addition, all the calls to the Knative Service are routed via the Istio ingress gateway; therefore you also need to know the IP address and port number of the service called `istio-ingressgateway` in the `istio-system` namespace.

For your convenience, we have added a script named *call.sh* (refer to the following listing) in the directory *$BOOK_HOME/bin*. It encapsulates all the logic that is needed to call the Knative Service:

```
#!/bin/bash

KSVC_NAME=${1:-'greeter'} ❶

IP_ADDRESS="$(minikube ip):$(kubectl get svc istio-ingressgateway \
  --namespace istio-system \
  --output 'jsonpath={.spec.ports[?(@.port==80)].nodePort}')" ❷

curl -H "Host:$KSVC_NAME.chapter-2.example.com" $IP_ADDRESS ❸
```

❶ The script defaults to a `ksvc` named `greeter`, unless another name is provided as a command-line parameter.

❷ The minikube IP address is retrieved using the command `minikube ip` (e.g., 192.168.99.100). The NodePort (*https://oreil.ly/mcWN8*) of the Istio ingress gateway service is also retrieved and appended to the IP_ADDRESS (e.g. 192.168.99.100:31380).

❸ The curl command uses the Knative Service URL via the Host header value.

The expanded curl command from the *call.sh* script will look something like the following:

```
curl -H "Host:greeter.chapter-2.example.com" 192.168.99.100:31380
```

Now, invoke the service by executing the script *$BOOK_HOME/bin/call.sh*:

```
$ $BOOK_HOME/bin/call.sh
Hi greeter => 9861675f8845 : 1
```

 You should notice that if your ksvc pod called greeter is not interacted with (i.e., not called/invoked), it will terminate as Knative Serving will automatically scale-to-zero any Knative Service pods that are not being actively used. If needed, *$BOOK_HOME/bin/call.sh* will wake up greeter, causing it to scale back up to an actively running pod. You can use watch kubectl get pods to monitor the pod lifecycle.

The deployment of the greeter service has also created a Knative Configuration. The Knative Configuration holds the current state of the Knative Service—that is, which revision of the service should receive the requests. Currently you should only have one revision named greeter-v1; therefore, running the command kubectl -n chapter-2 get configurations greeter should result in a single greeter configuration as shown here:

```
$ kubectl get configurations greeter
NAME      LATESTCREATED   LATESTREADY    READY
greeter   greeter-v1      greeter-v1     True
```

2.2 Updating a Knative Service Configuration

Problem

You need to update the configuration of your existing service but want to ensure the changes can be rolled back if needed.

Solution

Twelve-factor app principles state that any change to application configuration is considered a new revision. A *revision* is the immutable application and configuration state that gives you the capability to roll back to any last known good state.

Recall the Knative Service deployment model that we saw earlier in Figure 2-1. A ksvc creates a Configuration, which creates a Revision, which creates a Deployment, which creates a ReplicaSet, which creates the Pod that is your running service.

Any update to the application, such as a new container image, a tweaked liveness probe, or a change to an environment variable, will cause Knative to roll out a new revision. Every new revision rollout will create a new Kubernetes Deployment.

In this section, we will make a simple update to the application by adding an environment variable called MESSAGE_PREFIX to the Knative Service YAML. The following listing shows the updated Knative Service resource file with the environment variable added in its spec section:

```
apiVersion: serving.knative.dev/v1
kind: Service
metadata:
  name: greeter
spec:
  template:
    metadata:
      name: greeter-v2  ❶
    spec:
      containers:
      - image: quay.io/rhdevelopers/knative-tutorial-greeter:quarkus
        env:  ❷
        - name: MESSAGE_PREFIX
          value: Namaste
        livenessProbe:
          httpGet:
            path: /healthz
        readinessProbe:
          httpGet:
            path: /healthz
```

❶ The name of the Knative Service. To differentiate between the two revisions, we have called this one greeter-v2.

❷ An environment variable named MESSAGE_PREFIX with a value of Namaste. This environment variable will be used by the application when responding with the greeting.

To roll out this newly updated configuration, deploy the file called *service-env.yaml*:

```
$ kubectl -n chapter-2 apply -f service-env.yaml
```

This command will result in a new Kubernetes Deployment:

```
$ watch kubectl get deployments
NAME                   READY  UP-TO-DATE  AVAILABLE  AGE
greeter-v1-deployment  0/0    0           0          6m48s
greeter-v2-deployment  1/1    1           1          22s
```

Discussion

When you examine the Pods in the namespace `chapter-2`, you should only see one pod corresponding to `greeter-v2` running as shown in the following listing:

```
$ watch kubectl get pods
NAME                                    READY   STATUS    AGE
greeter-v2-deployment-9984bb56d-gn6tm   2/2     Running   15s
```

Your `greeter-v1` deployment had no requests for approximately 60 seconds, which is the Knative default scale-down time window. `greeter-v1` was automatically scaled down to zero since it lacked invocations. This is the key to how Knative Serving helps you save expensive cloud resources using serverless services. You will learn more about this feature in Chapter 3.

Any update to the Knative Service will create a new revision. You should now have two revisions of the Knative Service `greeter`. Run the following command to see the available revisions:

```
$ kubectl -n chapter-2 get revisions
```

You should see two revisions, each one associated with `greeter-v1` and `greeter-v2`, respectively. The following listing shows the available revisions for the `greeter` service:

```
NAME        CONFIG NAME   K8S SERVICE NAME   GENERATION   READY
greeter-v1  greeter       greeter-v1         1            True
greeter-v2  greeter       greeter-v2         2            True
```

This is a new revision rollout, so there will not be a new Route, ksvc, or Configuration created. You can verify the existing state of the Knative resources Route, ksvc, and Configuration by the running the following commands:

- `kubectl get routes`
- `kubectl get ksvc`
- `kubectl get configurations`

When you call the service you receive a response similar to Namaste greeter ⇒ *9861675f8845* : 1. Knative is now routing 100% of the end-user traffic to the new revision `greeter-v2`:

```
$ $BOOK_HOME/bin/call.sh
Namaste greeter => 9861675f8845 : 1
```

How does the Knative Route know which revision to send all the traffic to?

It uses the Knative Configuration, which is responsible for holding the state of a Knative Service—that is, how to distribute traffic between various revisions. By default, it routes 100% of the traffic to any newly created revision, which in this case is greeter-v2. To verify, run:

```
$ kubectl get configurations greeter
NAME      LATESTCREATED   LATESTREADY   READY
greeter   greeter-v2      greeter-v2    True
```

2.3 Distributing Traffic Between Knative Service Revisions

Problem

In a typical microservices deployment, you may wish to deploy applications using common deployment patterns such as Canary (*https://oreil.ly/WDJeA*) or blue-green (*https://oreil.ly/sMfOU*). To use these deployment patterns with Knative, you will need to have one or more revisions of the application to distribute the traffic.

Solution

The `traffic` block of the Knative Service resource YAML controls the distribution of traffic between multiple revisions.

The `traffic` block of the Knative Serving YAML describes the traffic distribution requirements. For example:

```
apiVersion: serving.knative.dev/v1
kind: Service
metadata:
  name: foo
spec:
  template:
     # removed for brevity
  traffic: ❶
  - tag: v1 ❷
    revisionName: foo-v1 ❸
    percent: 50 ❹
  - tag: v2
    revisionName: foo-v2
    percent: 50
```

❶ The `traffic` block to specify the traffic distribution

❷ The unique name for this traffic block list item

❸ The Knative Revision that will participate in the traffic distribution

❹ The amount of traffic that the revision will receive; it is a numerical value in percentage

Discussion

The traffic distribution is added using the `traffic` block in the Knative Service YAML. Each traffic block can define one or more items with following attributes:

tag
> An identifier for the traffic distribution. This tag will act as the prefix in the Knative Route to send traffic to this particular revision.

revisionName
> The name of the Knative Service Revision that will participate in the traffic distribution. You can get the revision names using the command `kubectl get revisions <ksvc name>`.

percent
> The amount of traffic that this revision will handle. This value should not be greater than 100. In this example, Knative will send 50% of the traffic to the revision `foo-v1` and 50% to revision `foo-v2`.

Knative Serving does create a unique service URL for each tag. You can query them using:

```
$ kubectl -n chapter-2 get ksvc greeter -oyaml \
  | yq r - 'status.traffic[*.url']
http://greeter-v1.chapter-2.example.com
http://greeter-v2.chapter-2.example.com
```

Though by default, Knative Service will route the percentage of traffic as defined by the tags of the `traffic` block—that is, *$BOOK_HOME*/call.sh `greeter`—but you can also call them directly using the respective tag URLs; e.g., *$BOOK_HOME*/call.sh `greeter-v1` or *$BOOK_HOME*/call.sh `greeter-v2`.

Now that you have seen how to distribute the traffic between Knative Revisions, we can move on to patterns like blue-green and Canary.

2.4 Applying the Blue-Green Deployment Pattern

Problem

You need to deploy a change of your application into production rapidly using the blue-green deployment (*https://oreil.ly/sMfOU*) pattern and strategy.

Solution

Knative offers a simple way of switching 100% of the traffic from one Knative Service Revision (blue) to another newly rolled out Revision (green). If the new Revision (e.g., green) has erroneous behavior, then it is easy to roll back the change.

As part of this recipe you will apply the blue-green deployment pattern with the Knative Service called greeter. You should have already deployed two revisions of greeter named greeter-v1 and greeter-v2 based on the previous recipes found in this chapter.

With the deployment of greeter-v2 you noticed that Knative automatically started to routing 100% of the traffic to greeter-v2. Now let's assume that we need to roll back greeter-v2 to greeter-v1 for some critical reason.

The following Knative Service YAML is identical to the previously deployed greeter-v2 except that we have added the traffic section to indicate that 100% of the traffic should be routed to greeter-v1:

```yaml
apiVersion: serving.knative.dev/v1
kind: Service
metadata:
  name: greeter
spec:
  template:
    metadata:
      name: greeter-v2
    spec:
      containers:
        - image: quay.io/rhdevelopers/knative-tutorial-greeter:quarkus
          env:
            - name: MESSAGE_PREFIX
              value: Namaste
          livenessProbe:
            httpGet:
              path: /healthz
          readinessProbe:
            httpGet:
              path: /healthz
  traffic:
    - tag: v1
      revisionName: greeter-v1
      percent: 100
    - tag: v2
      revisionName: greeter-v2
      percent: 0
    - tag: latest
      latestRevision: true
      percent: 0
```

Discussion

If you observe the resource YAML, we have added a special tag called latest. Since you have defined that 100% of the traffic needs to go to greeter-v1, this tag can be used to suppress the default behavior of the Knative Service to route 100% of the traffic to the latest revision.

Before you apply the resource *$BOOK_HOME/basics/service-pinned.yaml*, call the greeter service again to verify that it is still providing the response from greeter-v2 that includes Namaste:

```
$ $BOOK_HOME/bin/call.sh
Namaste  greeter => 9861675f8845 : 1
```

```
$ kubectl get pods
NAME                                         READY   STATUS    AGE
greeter-v2-deployment-9984bb56d-gr4gp        2/2     Running   14s
```

Now apply the updated Knative Service configuration using the command as shown in the following snippet:

```
kubectl -n chapter-2 apply -f service-pinned.yaml
```

You will notice that the command does not create any new Configuration/Revision/Deployment as there was no application update (e.g., image tag, environment variable, etc.), but when you call the service, Knative scales up the greeter-v1 and the service responds with the text Hi greeter ⇒ *9861675f8845* : 1.

```
$ $BOOK_HOME/bin/call.sh
Hi  greeter => 9861675f8845 : 1
```

```
$ kubectl get pods
NAME                                         READY   STATUS    AGE
greeter-v1-deployment-6f75dfd9d8-s5bvr       2/2     Running   5s
```

 As an exercise, flip all the traffic back to greeter-v2 (green). You need to edit the traffic block of the *service-pinned.yaml* and update the revision name to greeter-v2. After you redeploy the *service-pinned.yaml*, try calling the service again to notice the difference. If everything went smoothly you will notice the service calls will now go to only greeter-v2.

2.5 Applying the Canary Release Pattern

Problem

You need to deploy a change of your application into production rapidly, but you want only a fraction of the end-user traffic to flow to the changed version. This is known as a Canary release (*https://oreil.ly/WDJeA*).

Solution

A Canary release is more effective when you want to reduce the risk of introducing new features. It provides you with a better feature-feedback loop before rolling out the change to your entire user base.

Knative allows you to split the traffic between revisions in increments as small as 1%.

To see this in action, apply the following Knative Service definition that will split the traffic 80% to 20% between greeter-v1 and greeter-v2:

```
apiVersion: serving.knative.dev/v1
kind: Service
metadata:
  name: greeter
spec:
  template:
    metadata:
      name: greeter-v2
    spec:
      containers:
        - image: quay.io/rhdevelopers/knative-tutorial-greeter:quarkus
          env:
            - name: MESSAGE_PREFIX
              value: Namaste
          livenessProbe:
            httpGet:
              path: /healthz
          readinessProbe:
            httpGet:
              path: /healthz
  traffic:
    - tag: v1
      revisionName: greeter-v1
      percent: 80
    - tag: v2
      revisionName: greeter-v2
      percent: 20
    - tag: latest
      latestRevision: true
      percent: 0
```

To roll out the greeter Canary deployment, use the following command:

```
$ kubectl -n chapter-2 apply -f service-canary.yaml
```

Discussion

As in the previous section on deployments in Recipe 2.4, the command will not create any new Configuration/Revision/Deployment. To observe the traffic distribution you need to run the script *$BOOK_HOME/bin/poll.sh*, which is almost identical to *$BOOK_HOME/bin/call.sh* but will invoke the Knative Service in a loop:

```
$ $BOOK_HOME/bin/poll.sh
```

With the *poll.sh* script running you will see that approximately 80% of the responses are returned from `greeter-v1` and approximately 20% from `greeter-v2`. See the following listing for sample output:

```
Hi  greeter => 9861675f8845 : 1
Hi  greeter => 9861675f8845 : 2
Namaste  greeter => 9861675f8845 : 1
Hi  greeter => 9861675f8845 : 3
Hi  greeter => 9861675f8845 : 4
Hi  greeter => 9861675f8845 : 5
Hi  greeter => 9861675f8845 : 6
Hi  greeter => 9861675f8845 : 7
Hi  greeter => 9861675f8845 : 8
Hi  greeter => 9861675f8845 : 9
Hi  greeter => 9861675f8845 : 10
Hi  greeter => 9861675f8845 : 11
Namaste  greeter => 9861675f8845 : 2
Hi  greeter => 9861675f8845 : 12
Hi  greeter => 9861675f8845 : 13
Hi  greeter => 9861675f8845 : 14
Hi  greeter => 9861675f8845 : 15
Hi  greeter => 9861675f8845 : 16
...
```

You should also notice that two pods are running representing both `greeter-v1` and `greeter-v2`:

```
$ watch kubectl get pods
NAME                                         READY   STATUS    AGE
greeter-v1-deployment-6f75dfd9d8-86q89       2/2     Running   12s
greeter-v2-deployment-9984bb56d-n7xvm        2/2     Running   2s
```

 As a challenge, adjust the traffic distribution and observe the responses while the *poll.sh* script is actively running.

You should now have an understanding of Knative Serving, the Knative Serving Deployment model, how Knative Serving aids in the deployment of your applications, and advanced deployment techniques like blue-green and Canary.

In the next chapter, we will take a deeper dive into Knative Serving's autoscaling capabilities.

CHAPTER 3

Autoscaling Knative Services

Serverless-style architecture is not only about terminating your services when they are not in use but also about scaling them up based on demand. Knative handles these requirements effectively using its *scale-to-zero* and *autoscaling* capabilities:

Scale-to-zero

After a time of idleness your Knative Serving Service's Revision is considered to be *inactive*. Knative will terminate all the pods that correspond to that inactive Revision, and the Routes for that inactive Revision will be mapped to Knative Serving's *activator* service. The activator becomes the endpoint for receiving and buffering your end-user's HTTP traffic, to allow for the autoscaler—that is, the Knative Service's ability to scale from zero to n pods—to do its job.

Autoscaling

Autoscaling is the ability for the Knative Service to scale out its pods based on inbound HTTP traffic. The autoscaling feature of Knative is managed by:

- Knative Horizontal Pod Autoscaler (KPA)
- Horizontal Pod Autoscaler (HPA); the default autoscaler built into Kubernetes

The HPA relies on three important metrics: *concurrency, requests per second*, and *cpu*. The KPA can be thought of as an extended version of the HPA with a few tweaks to the default HPA algorithms to make it more suited to handle the more dynamic and load-driven Knative scaling requirements.

With our current setup of a Kubernetes cluster with minikube, which is a smaller cluster with limited resources, it is easy to demonstrate the autoscaling using the `concurrency` metric. Hence, all the recipes in this chapter focus on the `concurrency` metric.

Before You Begin

All the recipes in this chapter will be executed from the directory *$BOOK_HOME/scaling*, so change to the recipe directory by running:

```
$ cd $BOOK_HOME/scaling
```

The recipes of this chapter will deployed in the `chapter-3` namespace, so switch to the `chapter-3` namespace with the following command:

```
$ kubectl config set-context --current --namespace=chapter-3
```

3.1 Configuring Knative Service for Autoscaling

Problem

You want understand how to configure Knative Serving for autoscaling.

Solution

All the scale-to-zero and autoscaling parameters are defined in a Kubernetes Config-Map called `config-autoscaler` in the `knative-serving` namespace. You can view the ConfigMap with a simple `kubectl` command:

```
$ kubectl -n knative-serving get cm config-autoscaler -o yaml
```

The following code snippet provides an abridged version of the `config-autoscaler` ConfigMap contents. We focus on the few properties that impact the recipes included in this chapter:

```
apiVersion: v1
data:
  container-concurrency-target-default: "100" ❶
  enable-scale-to-zero: "true" ❷
  stable-window: "60s" ❸
  scale-to-zero-grace-period: "30s" ❹
```

❶ The default container concurrency for each service pod; defaults to 100

❷ Flag to enable or disable scale down to zero; defaults to `true`

❸ The time period in which the requests are monitored for calls and metrics; defaults to 60 seconds

❹ The time period within which the inactive pods are terminated; defaults to 30 seconds

Discussion

Each Knative Service pod is configured to handle 100 concurrent requests from its clients. The property `container-concurrency-target-default` of the config-autoscaler ConfigMap is used to configure the concurrency for each service pod; when the concurrent requests reach this limit, Knative Serving will scale up additional pods to handle the excess load.

The scale-to-zero—that is, the ability of Knative to terminate the inactive pods—can be controlled by the property `enable-scale-to-zero`. The default is `true`, which instructs Knative to scale-to-zero the pod if it has not received requests within the `stable-window` interval. You disable scale-to-zero to by setting this property to `false`.

The `stable-window` is the time period in which the autoscaler is monitoring requests/metrics; if there are zero requests to a pod over the default 60 seconds, then the autoscaler will begin to scale-to-zero by setting it to `inactive`.

The `scale-to-zero-grace-period` is the time period in which the autoscaler is monitoring `inactive` pods and will attempt to terminate those pods.

The recipes in this chapter rely on the defaults and any overridden configuration will be seen as annotations on the Knative Serving Service YAML. Check config-autoscaler (*https://oreil.ly/CHrm4*) for a list of all possible autoscaling properties.

3.2 Observing Scale-to-Zero

Problem

You want to observe your Knative Service scaling down to zero.

Solution

After deployment of your Knative Service as described in Chapter 2, simply `watch` the pod lifecycle with the following command:

```
$ watch kubectl get pods
```

Use the `watch` command in a new terminal window, as that will allow you to observe the scale-to-zero and autoscaling from zero to N. You can monitor the AGE column of the pod to measure how long it takes to scale down. By default, it should happen shortly after 60 seconds but before 90 seconds.

If you have not deployed the `greeter` Knative Serving Service, run:

```
$ kubectl -n chapter-3 apply -f $BOOK_HOME/basics/service.yaml
service.serving.knative.dev/greeter created
```

Open a new terminal window and watch the pod lifecycle with the command:

```
$ watch kubectl get pods
NAME                                          READY   STATUS     AGE
greeter-v1-deployment-b8db5486c-jl9gv         2/2     Running    8s
```

And as you wait and watch, you will see the pod terminate:

```
NAME                                          READY   STATUS        AGE
greeter-v1-deployment-b8db5486c-jl9gv         2/2     Terminating   64s
```

To make sure the pod is up and running, use the script *call.sh*:

```
$ $BOOK_HOME/bin/call.sh
Hi  greeter => 9861675f8845 : 1
```

Discussion

The mapping from the actual service URL to the Knative activator URL is transparent and is not visible by viewing the Knative Route of the corresponding Knative Service. The reprogramming of the network from the actual service pod to the activator pod in `knative-serving` is asynchronous in nature, so the `scale-to-zero-grace-period` should provide enough slack for this to happen. Once the `stable-window scale-to-zero-grace-period` is exceeded, the Revision will be scaled-to-zero replicas and those pods will be terminated.

When another request targets an inactive Revision, the activator intercepts that request and will instruct the Knative autoscaler to create new pods for that service Revision.

Termination Period

The actual time that the autoscaler takes to terminate the unused pod—that is, the pod that does not receive a request within `stable-window`—is set to `inactive`, and the *termination period* is the sum of `stable-window` plus `scale-to-zero-grace-period`. Using the example configuration as explained in the previous section, the value of the termination period is 90 seconds.

3.3 Configuring Your Knative Service to Handle Request Spikes

Problem

You want to configure your Knative Service to handle sudden request spikes by changing the default concurrency setting.

Solution

In your Knative Serving Service YAML, you can add annotations that will override the default behavior and autoscaling parameters:

```
autoscaling.knative.dev/target: "10"
```

The following listing illustrates the Knative Service Revision Template that adds the container concurrency annotation to reconfigure it from the default 100 to 10:

```
apiVersion: serving.knative.dev/v1alpha1
kind: Service
metadata:
  name: prime-generator
spec:
  template:
    metadata:
      name: prime-generator-v1
      annotations:
        # Target 10 in-flight-requests per pod.
        autoscaling.knative.dev/target: "10" ❶
    spec:
      containers:
      - image: quay.io/rhdevelopers/prime-generator:v27-quarkus
        livenessProbe:
          httpGet:
            path: /healthz
        readinessProbe:
          httpGet:
            path: /healthz
```

❶ Configure the container concurrency to be 10

Discussion

By default, the Knative Service container concurrency is set to 100 requests per pod. With the autoscaling.knative.dev/target annotation you are now overriding that value to be 10. You may also set this value to 0, where Knative will autoconfigure the value. In the absence of the annotation autoscaling.knative.dev/target, Knative by default sets this value to be 0.

Since we need to simulate the slowness in response to observe autoscaling, the service that you will use for doing the load test is a prime number generator using the Sieve of Eratosthenes (*https://oreil.ly/E6BzJ*). The Sieve of Eratosthenes is one of the slowest and least optimal ways to compute prime numbers within a range. The application tries to spice up the slowness by adding memory load, which makes the Knative Service respond slowly, thereby allowing it to autoscale.

Navigate to the recipe directory *$BOOK_HOME/scaling* and run:

```
$ kubectl apply -n chapter-3 -f service-10.yaml
```

The very first deployment of a Knative Serving Service will automatically scale to a single pod; wait for that service pod to come up:

```
$ watch kubectl get -n chapter-3 pods
NAME                                             READY   STATUS    AGE
prime-generator-v1-deployment-7464d56df-zhxzw    2/2     Running   5s
```

You can test the `prime-generator` service by using the script *$BOOK_HOME/bin/call.sh* with the service name `prime-generator` as a parameter:

```
$ $BOOK_HOME/bin/call.sh prime-generator
Value should be greater than 1 but recevied 0
```

In order to verify your updated concurrency setting (e.g., `autoscaling.kna tive.dev/target: "10"`) you need to drive enough load into the system to observe its behavior.

Sending `50` concurrent requests will cause the Knative autoscaler to scale up 7 service pods. The formula to calculate the target number of pods is as follows:

```
number of pods = total number of requests / container-concurrency
```

In the sample code repository, we have provided a load testing script called *load.sh*, and it leverages a command-line utility called hey. Run the following command to send 50 concurrent requests to the `prime-generator` service:

```
#!/bin/bash

hey -c 50 -z 10s \  ❶
  -host "$HOST_HEADER" \  ❷
  "http://$IP_ADDRESS/?sleep=3&upto=10000&memload=100"  ❸
```

❶ Invoke the hey load testing tool with a concurrency of 50 requests and for a duration of 10 seconds

❷ As you did earlier, pass the `Host` header; in this case it will be `prime-generator.chapter-3.example.com`

❸ The request URL parameters:

`sleep`

> Simulates slow-performing operations so that the requests pile up by sleeping for 3 seconds

`upto`

> Calculates the prime number up to this maximum

`load`

> Simulates the memory load of `100 megabytes(mb)`

To watch the autoscaling in action, you should open two terminal windows, one to run the `watch` command `watch kubectl get pods -n chapter-3` and the other to run the load test script *$BOOK_HOME/bin/load.sh*.

```
$ $BOOK_HOME/bin/load.sh

$ watch kubectl get pods
NAME                                            READY   STATUS    AGE
prime-generator-v1-deployment-6b8c59c85b-2tnb9  2/2     Running   5s
prime-generator-v1-deployment-6b8c59c85b-52295  2/2     Running   9s
prime-generator-v1-deployment-6b8c59c85b-67jdm  2/2     Running   7s
prime-generator-v1-deployment-6b8c59c85b-dm4zm  2/2     Running   7s
prime-generator-v1-deployment-6b8c59c85b-fwghr  2/2     Running   7s
prime-generator-v1-deployment-6b8c59c85b-rfm97  2/2     Running   7s
prime-generator-v1-deployment-6b8c59c85b-trmtl  2/2     Running   3s
```

Based on the parameters provided to the load testing script and the value of `autoscaling.knative.dev/target: "10"`, you will see more than 7 pods springing to life.

If you continue watching the pod lifecycle and do not continue to send in load, you will see that Knative will aggressively start to terminate unneeded pods:

```
NAME                                            READY   STATUS       AGE
prime-generator-v1-deployment-6b8c59c85b-2tnb9  2/2     Terminating  66s
prime-generator-v1-deployment-6b8c59c85b-52295  2/2     Running      70s
prime-generator-v1-deployment-6b8c59c85b-67jdm  2/2     Terminating  68s
prime-generator-v1-deployment-6b8c59c85b-dm4zm  2/2     Terminating  68s
prime-generator-v1-deployment-6b8c59c85b-fwghr  2/2     Terminating  68s
prime-generator-v1-deployment-6b8c59c85b-rfm97  2/2     Terminating  68s
prime-generator-v1-deployment-6b8c59c85b-trmtl  2/2     Terminating  64s
```

3.4 Cold Start Latency

Problem

You want to avoid the wait time involved in scaling from zero to *n* pods based on request volume by setting a floor—a *minScale* number of pods. You may also want to set a ceiling—a *maxScale* number of pods.

Solution

The `minScale` and `maxScale` annotations on the Knative Service Template allow you to set limits on the minimum and maximum number of pods that can be scaled:

minScale

By default, Knative will scale-to-zero—that is, your service will scale-to-zero pods when no requests arrive within the `stable-window` time period. When the next requests come in, Knative will autoscale to the appropriate number of pods to handle those requests. This starting from zero and the associated wait time is known as *cold start latency*.

If your application needs to stay particularly responsive and/or has a long startup time, then it may be beneficial to keep a minimum number of pods always up. This technique is also called *pod warming*. With Knative Serving this is achieved by adding the annotation `autoscaling.knative.dev/minScale` to the Knative Service YAML.

maxScale

Knative by default does not set an upper limit to the number of pods. This means you are at risk of exceeding your computational resource limits. In order to mitigate the risk, Knative Serving allows you to add the annotation `autoscaling.knative.dev/maxScale` to the Knative Service YAML. With `maxScale` you can restrict the upper limit of the autoscaler.

In the following section you will set the `minScale` and `maxScale` on the Knative Service Revision Template and run a load test. You will notice that the autoscaling will max out at 5 pods and once the requests are responded to, it will scale down to 2 and not 0.

The following code snippet shows the Knative Service Revision Template with `minScale` and `maxScale` annotations configured:

```
apiVersion: serving.knative.dev/v1alpha1
kind: Service
metadata:
  name: prime-generator
spec:
  template:
    metadata:
      name: prime-generator-v2
      annotations:
        # the minimum number of pods to scale down to
        autoscaling.knative.dev/minScale: "2"  ❶
        # the maximum number of pods to scale up to
        autoscaling.knative.dev/maxScale: "5"  ❷
        # Target 10 in-flight-requests per pod.
        autoscaling.knative.dev/target: "10"
```

```
spec:
  containers:
    - image: quay.io/rhdevelopers/prime-generator:v27-quarkus
      livenessProbe:
        httpGet:
          path: /healthz
      readinessProbe:
        httpGet:
          path: /healthz
```

❶ The minimum number of pods is set to 2; these pods should always be available even after the Knative Service has exceeded the stable-window.

❷ The maximum number of pods is set to 5, the number of pods the service can scale up to when it receives more requests than its container concurrency limits.

To see these settings in action, first watch your pod lifecycle with the following command:

```
$ watch kubectl get pods
No resources found.
```

Depending on when you last invoked *call.sh* or *load.sh*, there should be no pods available as Knative would have terminated the inactive pods.

Now, apply an update to the prime-generator service that includes the minScale and maxScale annotations:

```
$ kubectl apply -n chapter-3 -f service-min-max-scale.yaml
```

You should see an immediate response in your watch kubectl get pods terminal as shown here:

```
$ watch kubectl get pods
NAME                                            READY   STATUS    AGE
prime-generator-v2-deployment-84f459b57f-8kp6m  2/2     Running   14s
prime-generator-v2-deployment-84f459b57f-rlrqt  2/2     Running   10s
```

Discussion

You will notice that the prime-generator has been scaled up to 2 replicas as described by the autoscaling.knative.dev/minScale value and those pods will not be automatically scaled down to zero even after the termination period.

The final test is to attempt to overload the service with too many requests by running the load test script *$BOOK_HOME/bin/load.sh*. You will observe that maxScale will limit the autoscaler to 5 pods:

```
$ $BOOK_HOME/bin/load.sh
```

```
$ watch kubectl get pods
NAME                                                READY   STATUS      AGE
prime-generator-v2-deployment-84f459b57f-6vxxx      2/2     Running     5s
prime-generator-v2-deployment-84f459b57f-8kp6m      2/2     Running     2m35s
prime-generator-v2-deployment-84f459b57f-8trh2      2/2     Running     5s
prime-generator-v2-deployment-84f459b57f-ldg8m      2/2     Running     5s
prime-generator-v2-deployment-84f459b57f-rlrqt      2/2     Running     2m39s
```

And if you wait long enough, without another spike in requests, Knative Serving will scale down the unwanted pods:

```
NAME                                                READY   STATUS        AGE
prime-generator-v2-deployment-84f459b57f-6vxxx      2/2     Terminating   68s
prime-generator-v2-deployment-84f459b57f-8kp6m      2/2     Running       10m
prime-generator-v2-deployment-84f459b57f-8trh2      2/2     Terminating   68s
prime-generator-v2-deployment-84f459b57f-ldg8m      2/2     Terminating   68s
prime-generator-v2-deployment-84f459b57f-rlrqt      2/2     Running       10m
```

In this chapter, you learned about Knative Serving autoscaling behaviors by observing the default configuration and behavior, overriding the default Knative Serving concurrency configuration, and addressing cold start latency and an unlimited upper boundary.

In the next chapter, you will learn how to make your Knative Service respond to external events, such as a message received at a message broker topic.

Knative Eventing

In this chapter, we present recipes that will help you get started with Knative Eventing. We will start with a high-level overview of the usage patterns and then drill down into specific steps to connect the various components together into end-to-end working examples.

As previously described in Chapter 1, Knative has two major subprojects: Serving and Eventing. With Serving you have dynamic autoscaling, including scaling down to zero pods, based on the absence of HTTP traffic load. With Eventing, you now have that same autoscaling capability but bridged into other protocols or from other sources beyond HTTP. For example, a barrage of messages flowing through an Apache Kafka topic can cause autoscaling of your Kubernetes-based service to handle those messages. Or perhaps a scheduled event via cron can cause your service to awake from its slumber and perform its duties.

CloudEvents

CloudEvents (*https://cloudevents.io*) is a specification for describing event data in a common way. An event might be produced by any number of sources (e.g., Kafka, S3, GCP PubSub, MQTT), and as a software developer, you want a common abstraction for all event inputs.

Usage Patterns

There are three primary usage patterns with Knative Eventing:

Source to Sink
> Source to Sink provides the simplest getting started experience with Knative Eventing. It provides single *Sink*—that is, event receiving service—with no

queuing, backpressure, and filtering. Source to Sink does not support replies, which means the response from the Sink Service is ignored. As shown in Figure 4-1, the responsibility of the Event Source is just to deliver the message without waiting for the response from the Sink; hence, it will be appropriate to compare Source to Sink to the *fire and forget* messaging pattern.

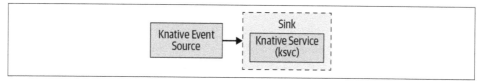

Figure 4-1. Source to Sink

Channels and Subscriptions

With *Channels* and *Subscriptions*, the Knative Eventing system defines a *Channel*, which can connect to various backends such as In-Memory, Kafka, and GCP PubSub for sourcing the events. Each Channel can have one or more Subscribers in the form of Sink Services as shown in Figure 4-2, which can receive the event messages and process them as needed. Each message from the Channel is formatted as a *CloudEvent* and sent further up in the chain to other Subscribers for further processing. The Channels and Subscriptions usage pattern does not have the ability to filter messages.

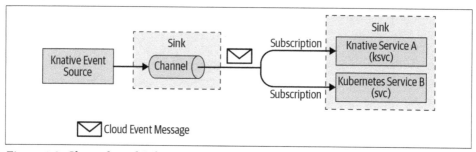

Figure 4-2. Channels and Subscriptions

Brokers and Triggers

Brokers and *Triggers* are similar to Channels and Subscriptions, except that they support filtering of events. Event filtering is a method that allows the Subscribers to show an interest in a certain set of messages that flows into the Broker. For each Broker, Knative Eventing will implicitly create a Knative Eventing Channel. As shown in Figure 4-3, the Trigger gets itself subscribed to the Broker and applies the filter on the messages on its subscribed Broker. The filters are applied on the CloudEvent attributes of the messages, before delivering the message to the interested Sink Services (Subscribers).

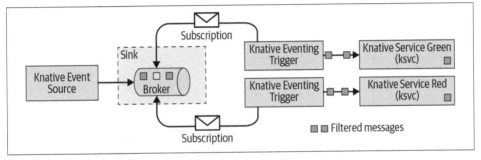

Figure 4-3. Brokers and Triggers

Before You Begin

All the recipes in this chapter will be executed from the directory
$BOOK_HOME/eventing, so change to the recipe directory by running:

```
$ cd $BOOK_HOME/eventing
```

The recipes in this chapter will be deployed in the chapter-4 namespace, so switch to
the chapter-4 namespace with the following command:

```
$ kubectl config set-context --current --namespace=chapter-4
```

The recipes in this chapter will enable us to do *eventing* with Knative and will help us
in understanding how Knative Serving Services can respond to external events via
Knative Eventing.

4.1 Producing Events with Eventing Sources

Problem

You need a way to connect to and receive events into your application.

Solution

Knative Eventing Sources are software components that emit events. The job of a
Source is to connect to, drain, capture, and potentially buffer events, often from an
external system, and then relay those events to the Sink.

Knative Eventing Sources install the following four sources out-of-the-box:

```
$ kubectl api-resources --api-group=sources.eventing.knative.dev
NAME                APIGROUP                      NAMESPACED   KIND
apiserversources    sources.eventing.knative.dev  true         ApiServerSource
containersources    sources.eventing.knative.dev  true         ContainerSource
cronjobsources      sources.eventing.knative.dev  true         CronJobSource
sinkbindings        sources.eventing.knative.dev  true         SinkBinding
```

Discussion

The `ApiServerSource` allows you to listen in on Kubernetes API events, like those events provided by `kubectl get events`.

The `ContainerSource` allows you to create your own container that emits events which can be targeted at Sinks—your specific Service.

The `CronJobSource` allows you to specify a cron timer, a recurring task that will emit an event to your Sink on a periodic basis. The `CronJobSource` is often the easiest way to verify that Knative Eventing is working properly.

`SinkBindings` allows you to link any addressable Kubernetes resource to receive events from any other Kubernetes resource that may produce events.

There are many other Source types, and you can review the current list of Sources (*https://oreil.ly/t33P7*) within the Knative documentation.

Before we take deep dive into the recipes in this chapter, let's quickly understand the structure of a Knative Event Source resource YAML:

```
apiVersion: sources.eventing.knative.dev/v1alpha1
kind: CronJobSource ❶
metadata:
  name: eventinghello-cronjob-source
spec: ❷
  schedule: "*/2 * * * *"
  data: '{"key": "every 2 mins"}'
  sink: ❸
    ref:
      apiVersion: serving.knative.dev/v1alpha1
      kind: Service
      name: eventinghello
```

❶ Knative Sources are described as CRDs; therefore, you construct an artifact with the correct kind

❷ spec will be unique per Source, per kind

❸ sink will be described next

4.2 Receiving Events with Knative Eventing Sinks

Problem

You need to connect your custom service to the events from an Event Source.

Solution

Knative Eventing Sink is how you specify the event receiver—that is, the consumer of the event. Sinks can be invoked directly in a point-to-point fashion by referencing them via the Event Source's `sink` as shown here:

```
apiVersion: sources.eventing.knative.dev/v1alpha1
kind: CronJobSource
metadata:
  name: eventinghello-cronjob-source
spec:
  schedule: "*/2 * * * *"
  data: '{"key": "every 2 mins"}'
  sink: ❶
    ref:
      apiVersion: serving.knative.dev/v1alpha1 ❷
      kind: Service
      name: eventinghello ❸
```

❶ `sink` can target any Kubernetes Service or

❷ a Knative Serving Service

❸ deployed as "eventinghello"

Discussion

The Sinks can target one of your Services—your code that will receive an HTTP POST with a CloudEvent payload. However, the Sink is also very flexible; it might point to a Channel (see Recipe 4.9 or a Broker (see Recipe 4.10), allowing for a publish-subscribe messaging pattern with one or more potential receivers. The Sink is often your Knative or Kubernetes Service that wishes to react to a particular event.

4.3 Deploying a Knative Eventing Service

Problem

Your Knative or Kubernetes Service needs to receive input from Knative Eventing in a generic fashion, as events may come from many potential sources.

Solution

Your code will handle an HTTP POST as shown in the following listing, where the CloudEvent data is available as HTTP headers as well as in the body of the request:

```
@PostMapping("/")
public ResponseEntity<String> myPost (
```

```
      HttpEntity<String> http) {

   System.out.println("ce-id=" + http.getHeaders().get("ce-id"));
   System.out.println("ce-source=" + http.getHeaders().get("ce-source"));
   System.out.println("ce-specversion=" + http.getHeaders()
                                      .get("ce-specversion"));
   System.out.println("ce-time=" + http.getHeaders().get("ce-time"));
   System.out.println("ce-type=" + http.getHeaders().get("ce-type"));
   System.out.println("content-type=" + http.getHeaders().getContentType());
   System.out.println("content-length=" + http.getHeaders().getContentLength());

   System.out.println("POST:" + http.getBody());
}
```

The CloudEvent SDK (*https://github.com/cloudevents*) provides a class library and framework integration for various language runtimes such as Go, Java, and Python.

Additional details on the CloudEvent to HTTP mapping (*https://oreil.ly/QaNIP*) can be found in the CloudEvent GitHub repository (*https://github.com/cloudevents/spec*).

The following listing shows a simple Knative Service (Sink):

```
apiVersion: serving.knative.dev/v1alpha1
kind: Service
metadata:
  name: eventinghello
spec:
  template:
    metadata:
      name: eventinghello-v1
      annotations:
        autoscaling.knative.dev/target: "1"❶
    spec:
      containers:
      - image: quay.io/rhdevelopers/eventinghello:0.0.1
```

❶ A concurrency of 1 HTTP request (an event) is consumed at a time. Most applications/services can easily handle many events concurrently and Knative's out-of-the-box default is 100. For the purposes of experimentation, it is interesting to see the behavior when you use 1 as the autoscaling target.

Discussion

You can deploy and verify that the eventinghello Sink Service has been deployed successfully by looking for READY marked as True:

```
$ kubectl -n chapter-4 apply -f eventing-hello-sink.yaml
service.serving.knative.dev/eventinghello created
$ kubectl get ksvc
NAME            URL                                           READY
eventinghello   http://eventinghello.myeventing.example.com   True
```

The default behavior of Knative Serving is that the very first deployment of a Knative Serving Service will automatically scale up to one pod, and after about 90 seconds it will autoscale down to zero pods.

You can actively watch the pod lifecycle with the following command:

```
$ watch kubectl get pods
```

You can monitor the logs of the eventinghello pod with:

```
$ stern eventinghello -c user-container
```

Wait until eventinghello scales to zero pods before moving on.

4.4 Connecting a Source to the Service

Problem

You have a Knative Serving Service (Sink) and need to connect it to a Knative Eventing Source to test its autoscaling behavior.

Solution

Deploy a CronJobSource, as it is the easiest solution to verify if Knative Eventing is responding to events correctly. To deploy a CronJobSource, run the following command:

```
$ kubectl -n chapter-4 apply -f eventinghello-source.yaml
cronjobsource.sources.eventing.knative.dev/eventinghello-cronjob-source created
$ kubectl -n chapter-4 get cronjobsource
NAME                            READY   AGE
eventinghello-cronjob-source    True    10s
```

Discussion

The deployment of a CronJobSource also produces a pod with a prefix of "cronjobsource-eventinghell" as shown:

```
$ watch kubectl get pods
NAME                                          READY   STATUS    AGE
cronjobsource-eventinghello-54b9ef12-2c2f-11ea  1/1     Running   14s
```

Based on our cron expression, after two minutes it will kick off an event that will cause the eventinghello pod to scale up as shown the following listing:

```
$ watch kubectl get pods
NAME                                          READY  STATUS    AGE
cronjobsource-eventinghell-54b9ef12-2c2f-11ea  1/1    Running   97s
eventinghello-v1-deployment-7cfcb664ff-r694p   2/2    Running   10s
```

After approximately 60 seconds, the `eventinghello` will autoscale down to zero pods, as it is a Knative Serving Service that will only be available while it is actively receiving events:

```
$ watch kubectl get pods
NAME                                           READY STATUS       AGE
cronjobsource-eventinghell-54b9ef12-2c2f-11ea  1/1   Running      2m28s
eventinghello-v1-deployment-7cfcb664ff-r694p   2/2   Terminating  65s
```

You can follow logs to see the CloudEvent details by using `stern`:

```
$ stern eventinghello -c user-container
ce-id=a1e0cbea-8f66-4fa6-8f3c-e5590c4ee147
ce-source=/apis/v1/namespaces/chapter-5/cronjobsources/
eventinghello-cronjob-source
ce-specversion=1.0
ce-time=2020-01-01T00:44:00.000889221Z
ce-type=dev.knative.cronjob.event
content-type=application/json
content-length=22
POST:{"key":"every 2 mins"}
```

Finally, when you are done with experimentation, simply delete the source and service:

```
$ kubectl -n chapter-4 delete -f eventinghello-source.yaml
cronjobsource.sources.eventing.knative.dev "eventinghello-cronjob-source" deleted
$ kubectl -n chapter-4 delete -f eventing-hello-sink.yaml
service.serving.knative.dev "eventinghello" deleted
$ kubectl get pods -n chapter-4
No resources found.
```

4.5 Deploying an Apache Kafka Cluster

Problem

You need to deploy an Apache Kafka cluster.

Solution

One of the easiest ways to deploy an Apache Kafka cluster is to use Strimzi (*https://strimzi.io*), an operator and set of CRDs that deploys Apache Kafka inside of a Kubernetes cluster.

Discussion

As part of the upcoming recipes in this chapter, we will be deploying a Knative Source (see Recipe 4.6) that will respond to Apache Kafka Topic messages (events). Before getting to those recipes, we need to first deploy Apache Kafka inside your Kubernetes cluster. The strimzi (*https://oreil.ly/5SCVG*) Kubernetes operator (*https://oreil.ly/cjoIL*) can be used to deploy the Apache Kafka cluster in your Kubernetes cluster.

Run the following command to create the `kafka` namespace and deploy Apache Kafka into it:

```
$ kubectl create namespace kafka
$ curl -L \
https://github.com/strimzi/strimzi-kafka-operator\
/releases/download/0.16.2/strimzi-cluster-operator-0.16.2.yaml \
  | sed 's/namespace: .*/namespace: kafka/' \
  | kubectl apply -f - -n kafka
```

Wait for the `strimzi-cluster-operator` to be running:

```
$ watch kubectl get pods -n kafka
NAME                                      READY STATUS   AGE
strimzi-cluster-operator-85f596bfc7-7dgds 1/1   Running  1m2s
```

The strimzi operator would have installed several Apache Kafka–related CRDs, which can be used to create Apache Kafka core resources such as a topic, users, connectors, etc. You can verify the CRDs that are available by querying `api-resources`:

```
$ kubectl api-resources --api-group=kafka.strimzi.io
kafkabridges.kafka.strimzi.io              2019-12-28T14:53:14Z
kafkaconnects.kafka.strimzi.io             2019-12-28T14:53:14Z
kafkaconnects2is.kafka.strimzi.io          2019-12-28T14:53:14Z
kafkamirrormakers.kafka.strimzi.io         2019-12-28T14:53:14Z
kafkas.kafka.strimzi.io                    2019-12-28T14:53:14Z
kafkatopics.kafka.strimzi.io               2019-12-28T14:53:14Z
kafkausers.kafka.strimzi.io                2019-12-28T14:53:14Z
```

Now with the Apache Kafka operator running, you can deploy and verify a single-node Apache Kakfa cluster by running the command:

```
$ kubectl -n kafka apply -f kafka-broker-my-cluster.yaml
kafka.kafka.strimzi.io/my-cluster created
$ watch kubectl get pods -n kafka
NAME                                          READY STATUS   AGE
my-cluster-entity-operator-7d677bdf7b-jpws7   3/3   Running  85s
my-cluster-kafka-0                            2/2   Running  110s
my-cluster-zookeeper-0                        2/2   Running  2m22s
strimzi-cluster-operator-85f596bfc7-7dgds     1/1   Running  4m22s
```

The Kubernetes CRD resource *$BOOK_HOME/eventing/kafka-broker-my-cluster.yaml* will deploy a single Zookeeper, Kafka Broker, and an Entity-Operator. The Entity-Operator is responsible for managing different custom resources such as KafkaTopic and KafkaUser.

Now that you have an Apache Kafka cluster deployed, you can create a Kafka Topic using the KafkaTopic CRD. The following listing shows how to create a Kafka Topic named `my-topic`:

```
apiVersion: kafka.strimzi.io/v1alpha1
kind: KafkaTopic
metadata:
  name: my-topic
  labels:
    strimzi.io/cluster: my-cluster
spec:
  partitions: 10 ❶
  replicas: 1
```

❶ `partitions`: *n* allows for more concurrent scale-out of Sink pods. In theory, up to 10 pods will scale-up if there are enough messages flowing through the Kafka Topic.

 You can choose to skip the manual pre-creation of a KafkaTopic but the automatically generated topics will have partitions set to 1 by default.

Create and verify the topic:

```
$ kubectl -n kafka create -f kafka-topic-my-topic.yaml
kafkatopic.kafka.strimzi.io/my-topic created
$ kubectl -n kafka  get kafkatopics
NAME       PARTITIONS   REPLICATION FACTOR
my-topic   10           1
```

Verify that your Kafka Topic is working correctly by connecting a simple producer and consumer and creating some test messages. The sample code repository includes a script for producing Kafka messages called *kafka-producer.sh*. Execute the script and type in **one**, **two**, **three**, hitting Enter/Return after each string:

Producer

```
$ $BOOK_HOME/bin/kafka-producer.sh
>one
>two
>three
```

Consumer

You should also leverage the sample code repository's *kafka-consumer.sh* script to see the message flow through the topic. Open a new terminal and run:

```
$ $BOOK_HOME/bin/kafka-consumer.sh
one
two
three
```

You can use Ctrl-C to stop producer and consumer interaction and their associated pods.

4.6 Sourcing Apache Kafka Events with Knative Eventing

Problem

You wish to connect to an Apache Kafka cluster and have those messages flow through Knative Eventing.

Solution

Use the Knative Eventing KafkaSource to have the Kafka messages flow through the Knative Eventing Channels. You can deploy the Knative KafkaSource by running the command:

```
$ kubectl apply \
-f https://github.com/knative/eventing-contrib/\
releases/download/v0.12.2/kafka-source.yaml
```

The previous step deploys the Knative KafkaSource in the knative-sources name-space as well as a CRD, ServiceAccount, ClusterRole, etc. Verify that the Knative Source namespace includes the kafka-controller-manager-0 pod:

```
$ watch kubectl get pods -n knative-sources
NAME                          READY   STATUS    AGE
kafka-controller-manager-0    1/1     Running   1m17s
```

You should also deploy the Knative Kafka Channel that can be used to connect the Knative Eventing Channel with an Apache Kafka cluster backend. To deploy a Knative Kafka Channel, run:

```
$ curl -L "https://github.com/knative/eventing-contrib/\
releases/download/v0.12.2/kafka-channel.yaml" \
 | sed 's/REPLACE_WITH_CLUSTER_URL/my-cluster-kafka-bootstrap.kafka:9092/' \
 | kubectl apply --filename -
```

 "my-cluster-kafka-bootstrap.kafka:9092" comes from kubectl get services -n kafka.

Discussion

Look for three new pods in the knative-eventing namespace with the prefix "kafka":

```
$ watch kubectl get pods -n knative-eventing
NAME                                    READY   STATUS    AGE
eventing-controller-666b79d867-kq8cc    1/1     Running   64m
eventing-webhook-5867c98d9b-hzctw       1/1     Running   64m
imc-controller-7c4f9945d7-s59xd         1/1     Running   64m
imc-dispatcher-7b55b86649-nsjm2         1/1     Running   64m
kafka-ch-controller-7c596b6b55-fzxcx    1/1     Running   33s
kafka-ch-dispatcher-577958f994-4f2qs    1/1     Running   33s
kafka-webhook-74bbd99f5c-c84ls          1/1     Running   33s
sources-controller-694f8df9c4-pss2w     1/1     Running   64m
```

And you should also find some new api-resources as shown here:

```
$ kubectl api-resources --api-group=sources.eventing.knative.dev
NAME                APIGROUP                        NAMESPACED   KIND
apiserversources    sources.eventing.knative.dev    true         ApiServerSource
containersources    sources.eventing.knative.dev    true         ContainerSource
cronjobsources      sources.eventing.knative.dev    true         CronJobSource
kafkasources        sources.eventing.knative.dev    true         KafkaSource
sinkbindings        sources.eventing.knative.dev    true         SinkBinding
```

```
$kubectl api-resources --api-group=messaging.knative.dev
NAME                SHORTNAMES   APIGROUP                  NAMESPACED   KIND
channels            ch           messaging.knative.dev     true         Channel
inmemorychannels    imc          messaging.knative.dev     true         InMemoryChannel
kafkachannels       kc           messaging.knative.dev     true         KafkaChannel
parallels                        messaging.knative.dev     true         Parallel
sequences                        messaging.knative.dev     true         Sequence
subscriptions       sub          messaging.knative.dev     true         Subscription
```

Now that all of your infrastructure is configured, you can deploy the Knative Serving Service (Sink) by running the command:

```
$ kubectl apply -n chapter-5 -f eventing-hello-sink.yaml
service.serving.knative.dev/eventinghello created
$ kubectl get ksvc
NAME            URL                                       READY
eventinghello   http://eventinghello.kafka.example.com    True
```

Make sure to follow the logs using stern:

```
$ stern eventinghello -c user-container
```

The initial deployment of eventinghello will cause it to scale up to one pod. It will be around until it hits its scale-down time limit. Allow it to scale down to zero pods before continuing.

Create a KafkaSource for my-topic by connecting your Kafka Topic my-topic to eventinghello:

```
apiVersion: sources.eventing.knative.dev/v1alpha1
kind: KafkaSource
metadata:
  name: mykafka-source
spec:
  consumerGroup: knative-group
  bootstrapServers: my-cluster-kafka-bootstrap.kafka:9092 ❶
  topics: my-topic
  sink: ❷
    ref:
      apiVersion: serving.knative.dev/v1alpha1
      kind: Service
      name: eventinghello
```

❶ "my-cluster-kafka-bootstrap.kafka:9092" can be found via kubectl get -n kafka services

❷ This is another example of a direct Source to Service

The deployment of KafkaSource will result in a new pod prefixed with "mykafka-source":

```
$ kubectl -n chapter-4 apply -f mykafka-source.yaml
kafkasource.sources.eventing.knative.dev/mykafka-source created
$ watch kubectl get pods
NAME                                       READY  STATUS   RESTARTS  AGE
mykafka-source-vxs2k-56548756cc-j7m7v      1/1    Running  0         11s
```

Since we had test messages of "one," "two," and "three" from earlier, you might see the eventinghello service awaken to process those messages.

Wait for eventinghello to scale down to zero pods before moving on, and then push more Kafka messages into my-topic.

Let's now start an Apache Kafka producer that will send a message to my-topic:

```
$ $BOOK_HOME/bin/kafka-producer.sh
```

And then enter the following JSON-formatted messages:

```
{"hello":"world"}
```

```
{"hola":"mundo"}
```

```
{"bonjour":"le monde"}
```

```
{"hey": "duniya"}
```

Knative Eventing events through the KafkaSource must be JSON-formatted.

While making sure to monitor the logs of the eventinghello pod:

```
$ stern eventinghello -c user-container

ce-id=partition:1/offset:1
ce-source=/apis/v1/namespaces/kafka/kafkasources/mykafka-source#my-topic
ce-specversion=1.0
ce-time=2020-01-01T01:16:12.886Z
ce-type=dev.knative.kafka.event
content-type=application/json
content-length=17
POST:{"hey": "duniya"}
```

 The sample output has been modified for readability and formatting reasons. You can see the logging output of all your JSON-based event input in the terminal where you are watching the eventinghello logs.

4.7 Autoscaling with Apache Kafka and Knative Eventing

Problem

Now that you have a connected a Kafka Topic to Knative Eventing, you wish to see it scale out to greater than a single pod.

Solution

You simply need to set the autoscaling target low enough by adding the annotation autoscaling.knative.dev/target: "1", while simultaneously pushing enough messages through the topic. You have already set the target to be 1 when deploying the eventinghello sink as shown in the following listing:

```
apiVersion: serving.knative.dev/v1alpha1
kind: Service
metadata:
  name: eventinghello
spec:
  template:
    metadata:
      name: eventinghello-v1
      annotations:
        autoscaling.knative.dev/target: "1" ❶
```

```
  spec:
    containers:
    - image: quay.io/rhdevelopers/eventinghello:0.0.1
```

❶ The Knative Serving Sink Service was defined with the `autoscaling` annotation that limits concurrency to approximately one pod per event (Kafka message)

Discussion

With a concurrency factor of 1, if you are able to push in a number of Kafka message rapidly, you will see more than one `eventinghello` pod scaled up to handle the load.

You simply need an application that allows you to push in messages rapidly. Launch the Kafka Spammer (*https://oreil.ly/kW-wm*) application and push in at least three messages, then run the following command to start the `kafka-spammer` pod:

```
$ kubectl -n kafka run kafka-spammer \
  --image=quay.io/rhdevelopers/kafkaspammer:1.0.2
```

You then exec into the running `kafka-spammer` pod by running the following command:

```
$ KAFKA_SPAMMER_POD=$(kubectl -n kafka get pod -l "run=kafka-spammer" \
  -o jsonpath={.items[0].metadata.name})
$ kubectl -n kafka exec -it $KAFKA_SPAMMER_POD -- /bin/sh
```

Use curl to send in three messages:

```
$ curl localhost:8080/3
```

You should see about three `eventinghello` pods coming to life, as shown in the following listing:

```
$ watch kubectl get pods
NAME                                             READY  STATUS   AGE
eventinghello-v1-deployment-65c9b9c7df-8rwqc     1/2    Running  6s
eventinghello-v1-deployment-65c9b9c7df-q7pcf     1/2    Running  4s
eventinghello-v1-deployment-65c9b9c7df-zht2t     1/2    Running  6s
kafka-spammer-77ccd4f9c6-sx5j4                   1/1    Running  26s
my-cluster-entity-operator-7d677bdf7b-jpws7      3/3    Running  27m
my-cluster-kafka-0                               2/2    Running  27m
my-cluster-zookeeper-0                           2/2    Running  28m
mykafka-source-vxs2k-56548756cc-j7m7v            1/1    Running  5m12s
strimzi-cluster-operator-85f596bfc7-7dgds        1/1    Running  30m
```

The events are *not* being evenly distributed across the various `eventinghello` pods; the first pod up starts consuming them all immediately.

To close out the spammer, use `exit` and then delete its deployment:

```
$ kubectl delete -n kafka deployment kafka-spammer
```

4.8 Using a Kafka Channel as the Default Knative Channel

Problem

You want to use Apache Kafka as the default Channel backend for Knative Eventing.

Solution

Persistence and Durability (*https://oreil.ly/lFNs9*) are two very important features of any messaging-based architecture. The Knative Channel has built-in support for durability. Durability of messages becomes ineffective if the Knative Eventing Channel does not support persistence. Without persistence, it will not be able to deliver the messages to Subscribers that might be offline at the time of message delivery.

By default all Knative Channels created by the Knative Eventing API use InMemory-Channel (IMC), which does not have the capability to persist messages. To enable persistence we need to use one of the supported Channels (*https://oreil.ly/Er9RB*) such as GCP PubSub, Kafka, or Neural Autonomic Transport System (NATS) as the default Knative Channel backend.

We installed Apache Kafka earlier in Recipe 4.6. Let's now configure it to be the default Knative Channel backend:

```
apiVersion: v1
kind: ConfigMap
metadata:
  name: default-ch-webhook
  namespace: knative-eventing
data:
  default-ch-config: |
    clusterDefault: ❶
      apiVersion: messaging.knative.dev/v1alpha1
      kind: InMemoryChannel
    namespaceDefaults: ❷
      chapter-4:
        apiVersion: messaging.knative.dev/v1alpha1
        kind: KafkaChannel
        spec:
          numPartitions: 1
          replicationFactor: 1
```

❶   For the cluster we will still use the default InMemoryChannel

❷ For the namespace `chapter-4`, all Knative Eventing Channels will use `KafkaChannel` as the default

Run the following command to apply the Knative Eventing Channel configuration:

```
$ kubectl apply -f default-kafka-channel.yaml
```

Discussion

Since you have now made all Knative Eventing Channels of `chapter-4` to be Kafka-Channel, creating a Knative Eventing Channel in the `chapter-4` namespace will result in a corresponding Kafka Topic being created. Let's now verify it by creating a sample Channel as shown in the following listing:

```
cat <<EOF | kubectl apply -f -
apiVersion: messaging.knative.dev/v1alpha1
kind: Channel
metadata:
  name: my-events-ch
  namespace: chapter-4
spec: {}
EOF
```

When you now list the topics that are available in Kafka using the script *$BOOK_HOME/bin/kafka-list-topics.sh*, you should see a topic corresponding to your Channel `my-events-ch`:

```
$ $BOOK_HOME/bin/kafka-list-topics.sh
knative-messaging-kafka.chapter-4.my-events-ch
```

For each Knative Eventing Channel that you create, a Kafka Topic will be created. The topic's name will follow a convention like `knative-messaging-kafka.<your-channel-namespace>.<your-channel-name>`.

4.9 Using Knative Channels and Subscriptions

Problem

You would like to have multiple Sinks with potentially many services responding to events.

Solution

Use Knative Eventing Channels and Subscriptions:

Channels

Channels are an event-forwarding and persistence layer where each Channel is a separate Kubernetes Custom Resource. A Channel may be backed by Apache Kafka or InMemoryChannel.

Subscriptions

Subscriptions are how you register your service to listen to a particular channel.

The use of Channels and Subscriptions allows you to decouple the producers and consumers of events.

The recipe is as follows:

1. Create a Channel

2. Create a Source to Sink to the Channel

3. Create at least two Sink Services

4. Create Subscriptions to register your Sink Services with the Channel

Create a Channel:

```
apiVersion: messaging.knative.dev/v1alpha1
kind: Channel
metadata:
  name: eventinghello-ch
```

Verify that your Channel was created successfully:

```
$ kubectl -n chapter-4 create -f eventinghello-channel.yaml
channel.messaging.knative.dev/eventinghello-ch created
$ kubectl get ch
NAME                   READY
eventinghello-ch True
URL
http://eventinghello-ch-kn-channel.chapter-5.svc.cluster.local
```

Then you need to create a Source that will send events to the Channel:

```
apiVersion: sources.eventing.knative.dev/v1alpha1
kind: CronJobSource
metadata:
  name: my-cjs
spec:
  schedule: "*/2 * * * *"
  data: '{"message": "From CronJob Source"}'
  sink:
   ref:
    apiVersion: messaging.knative.dev/v1alpha1  ❶
    kind: Channel  ❷
    name: eventinghello-ch
```

❶ The Channel API is in the api-group `messaging.eventing.knative.dev`

❷ `kind` is a `Channel` instead of direct to a specific service; the default is an InMemoryChannel implementation

Deploy and verify that your `CronJobSource` is running:

```
$ kubectl -n chapter-4 create -f eventinghello-source-ch.yaml
cronjobsource.sources.eventing.knative.dev/my-cjs created
$ kubectl -n chapter-4 get cronjobsource
NAME      READY   AGE
my-cjs    True    8s
```

Now you create the Sink services that will become the Subscribers:

```
apiVersion: serving.knative.dev/v1alpha1
kind: Service
metadata:
  name: eventinghelloa
spec:
  template:
    metadata:
      name: eventinghelloa-v1  ❶
      annotations:
        autoscaling.knative.dev/target: "1"
    spec:
      containers:
      - image: quay.io/rhdevelopers/eventinghello:0.0.1
```

❶ The string `eventinghelloa` will help you identify this particular service:

```
apiVersion: serving.knative.dev/v1alpha1
kind: Service
metadata:
  name: eventinghellob
spec:
  template:
    metadata:
      name: eventinghellob-v1  ❶
      annotations:
        autoscaling.knative.dev/target: "1"
    spec:
      containers:
      - image: quay.io/rhdevelopers/eventinghello:0.0.1
```

❶ The string `eventinghellob` will help you identify this particular service:

```
$ kubectl -n chapter-4 create -f eventing-helloa-sink.yaml
service.serving.knative.dev/eventinghelloa created
$ kubectl -n chapter-4 create -f eventing-hellob-sink.yaml
service.serving.knative.dev/eventinghellob created
```

Now create the appropriate Subscription for `eventinghelloa` to the Channel `eventinghello-ch`:

```
apiVersion: messaging.knative.dev/v1alpha1
kind: Subscription
metadata:
  name: eventinghelloa-sub
spec:
  channel:
    apiVersion: messaging.knative.dev/v1alpha1
    kind: Channel
    name: eventinghello-ch
  subscriber:
    ref:
      apiVersion: serving.knative.dev/v1alpha1
      kind: Service
      name: eventinghelloa
```

And create the appropriate Subscription for `eventinghellob` to the Channel `eventinghello-ch`:

```
apiVersion: messaging.knative.dev/v1alpha1
kind: Subscription
metadata:
  name: eventinghellob-sub
spec:
  channel:
    apiVersion: messaging.knative.dev/v1alpha1
    kind: Channel
    name: eventinghello-ch
  subscriber:
    ref:
      apiVersion: serving.knative.dev/v1alpha1
      kind: Service
      name: eventinghellob
```

```
$ kubectl -n chapter-4 create -f eventing-helloa-sub.yaml
subscription.messaging.knative.dev/eventinghelloa-sub created
$ kubectl -n chapter-4 create -f eventing-hellob-sub.yaml
subscription.messaging.knative.dev/eventinghellob-sub created
```

Discussion

If you wait approximately two minutes for the `CronJobSource`, you will see both `eventinghelloa` and `eventinghellob` begin to run:

```
$ watch kubectl get pods
NAME                                                       READY STATUS  AGE
cronjobsource-my-cjs-93544f14-2bf9-11ea-83c7-08002737670c  1/1   Running 2m15s
eventinghelloa-1-deployment-d86bf4847-hvbk6                2/2   Running 5s
eventinghellob-1-deployment-5c986c7586-4clpb               2/2   Running 5s
```

Once you are done with your experimentation, you can delete the event source `my-cjs` and `eventinghelloa` and `eventinghellob`:

```
$ kubectl -n chapter-4 delete -f eventing-helloa-sink.yaml
$ kubectl -n chapter-4 delete -f eventing-helloa-sub.yaml
$ kubectl -n chapter-4 delete -f eventing-hellob-sink.yaml
$ kubectl -n chapter-4 delete -f eventing-hellob-sub.yaml
$ kubectl -n chapter-4 delete -f eventinghello-source-ch.yaml
```

4.10 Using Knative Eventing Brokers and Triggers

Problem

You need event filtering because, by default, all the events flowing through a Channel will be sent to all Subscribers. In some cases, the Subscriber wishes to receive only a set of messages based on certain criteria.

Solution

Use the Knative Eventing `Broker` and `Trigger` Custom Resources to allow for CloudEvent attribute filtering.

The recipe is as follows:

1. Inject the default Broker

2. Create at least two Sink Services

3. Create Triggers to register your Sink Services with the Channel

4. Push some events

Labeling the `chapter-4` namespace with `knative-eventing-injection=enabled` as shown in the following code will make Knative Eventing deploy a default Knative Eventing Broker and its related ingress:

```
$ kubectl label namespace chapter-4 knative-eventing-injection=enabled
```

Verify that the default Broker is running:

```
$ kubectl --namespace chapter-4 get broker
NAME     READY REASON URL                                                AGE
default  True          http://default-broker.chapter-4.svc.cluster.local  22s
```

This will also start two additional pods named `default-broker-filter` and `default-broker-ingress`:

```
$ watch kubectl get pods
NAME                                        READY STATUS   AGE
default-broker-filter-c6654bccf-qb272       1/1   Running  18s
default-broker-ingress-7479966dc7-99xvm     1/1   Running  18s
```

Now that you have the Broker configured, you need to create the Sinks eventing aloha and eventingbonjour, which will receive the filtered events.

Run the following command to deploy and verify the Knative Serving Services eventingaloha and eventingbonjour:

```
$ kubectl -n chapter-4 create -f eventing-aloha-sink.yaml
service.serving.knative.dev/eventingaloha created
$ kubectl -n chapter-4 create -f eventing-bonjour-sink.yaml
service.serving.knative.dev/eventingbonjour created
$ kubectl get ksvc
NAME                URL                                              READY
eventingaloha       http://eventingaloha.myeventing.example.com      True
eventingbonjour     http://eventingbonjour.myeventing.example.com    True
```

 The image being used by both of these services is identical. However, the difference between the names aloha and bonjour will make obvious which one is receiving a particular event.

```
$ watch kubectl get pods
NAME                                            READY   STATUS    AGE
default-broker-filter-c6654bccf-6448v           1/1     Running   8m40s
default-broker-ingress-74b49c78f4-mnskg         1/1     Running   8m40s
eventingaloha-v1-deployment-9b46d459b-f8pfr     2/2     Running   30s
eventingbonjour-v1-deployment-fcd46b4dc-x6wvc   2/2     Running   18s
```

Wait approximately 60 seconds for eventingaloha and eventingbonjour to terminate and scale down to zero before proceeding.

Now create the Trigger for eventingaloha that will associate the filtered events to a service:

```
apiVersion: eventing.knative.dev/v1alpha1
kind: Trigger
metadata:
  name: helloaloha
spec:
  filter:
    attributes:
      type: greeting ❶
  subscriber:
    ref:
      apiVersion: serving.knative.dev/v1alpha1
      kind: Service
      name: eventingaloha
```

❶ The type is the CloudEvent type that is mapped to the ce-type HTTP header. A Trigger can filter by CloudEvent attributes such as type, source, or extension.

Now create the Trigger for `eventingbonjour` that will associate the filtered events to a service:

```
apiVersion: eventing.knative.dev/v1alpha1
kind: Trigger
metadata:
  name: hellobonjour
spec:
  filter:
    attributes:
      type: greeting
  subscriber:
    ref:
      apiVersion: serving.knative.dev/v1alpha1
      kind: Service
      name: eventingbonjour
```

Verify that your Triggers are ready:

```
$ kubectl -n chapter-4 create -f trigger-helloaloha.yaml
trigger.eventing.knative.dev/helloaloha created
$ kubectl -n chapter-4 create -f trigger-hellobonjour.yaml
trigger.eventing.knative.dev/hellobonjour created
$ kubectl get triggers
NAME          READY BROKER   SUBSCRIBER_URI                                       AGE
helloaloha    True  default  http://eventingaloha.chapter-4.svc.cluster.local    24s
hellobonjour True  default  http://eventingbonjour.chapter-4.svc.cluster.local  48s
```

The preceding output has been modified for formatting purposes.

Discussion

Pull out the `subscriberURI` for `eventhingaloha`:

```
$ kubectl get trigger helloaloha -o jsonpath={.status.subscriberURI}
http://eventingaloha.chapter-4.svc.cluster.local
```

Pull out the `subscriberURI` for `eventhingbonjour`:

```
$ kubectl get trigger hellobonjour -o jsonpath={.status.subscriberURI}
http://eventingbonjour.chapter-4.svc.cluster.local
```

As well as the Broker's `subscriberURI`:

```
$ kubectl get broker default -o jsonpath={.status.address.url}
http://default-broker.chapter-4.svc.cluster.local
```

You should notice that the subscriberURIs are Kubernetes services with the suffix of chapter-4.svc.cluster.local. This means they can be interacted with from another pod within the Kubernetes cluster.

Now that you have set up the Brokers and Triggers, you need to send in some test messages to see the behavior:

First, start streaming the logs for the event consumers:

```
$ stern eventing -c user-container
```

Then create a pod for using the curl command:

```
apiVersion: v1
kind: Pod
metadata:
  labels:
    run: curler
  name: curler
spec:
  containers:
  - name: curler
    image: fedora:29  ❶
    tty: true
```

❶ You can use any image that includes a curl command.

Then exec into the curler pod:

```
$ kubectl -n chapter-4 apply -f curler.yaml
pod/curler created
$ kubectl -n chapter-4 exec -it curler -- /bin/bash
```

Using the curler pod's shell, curl the subcriberURI for eventingaloha:

```
$ curl -v "http://eventingaloha.chapter-4.svc.cluster.local" \
-X POST \
-H "Ce-Id: say-hello" \
-H "Ce-Specversion: 1.0" \
-H "Ce-Type: aloha" \
-H "Ce-Source: mycurl" \
-H "Content-Type: application/json" \
-d {"key":"from a curl"}
```

You will then see eventingaloha will scale-up to respond to that event:

```
$ watch kubectl get pods
NAME                                         READY STATUS   AGE
curler                                        1/1  Running  59s
default-broker-filter-c6654bccf-vxm5m         1/1  Running  11m
default-broker-ingress-7479966dc7-pvtx6       1/1  Running  11m
eventingaloha-1-deployment-6cdc888d9d-9xnnn   2/2  Running  30s
```

Next, curl the subcriberURI for eventingbonjour:

```
$ curl -v "http://eventingbonjour.chapter-4.svc.cluster.local" \
-X POST \
-H "Ce-Id: say-hello" \
-H "Ce-Specversion: 1.0" \
-H "Ce-Type: bonjour" \
-H "Ce-Source: mycurl" \
-H "Content-Type: application/json" \
-d {"key":"from a curl"}
```

And you will see the eventingbonjour pod scale up:

```
$ watch kubectl get pods
NAME                                         READY STATUS  AGE
curler                                       1/1   Running 82s
default-broker-filter-c6654bccf-vxm5m        1/1   Running 11m
default-broker-ingress-7479966dc7-pvtx6      1/1   Running 11m
eventingaloha-1-deployment-6cdc888d9d-9xnnn  2/2   Running 53s
eventingbonjour-1-deployment-fc7858b5b-s9prj 2/2   Running 5s
```

Now, trigger both eventingaloha and eventingbonjour by curling the subcriberURI
for the Broker:

```
$ curl -v "http://default-broker.chapter-4.svc.cluster.local" \
-X POST \
-H "Ce-Id: say-hello" \
-H "Ce-Specversion: 1.0" \
-H "Ce-Type: greeting" \
-H "Ce-Source: mycurl" \
-H "Content-Type: application/json" \
-d {"key":"from a curl"}
```

"Ce-Type: greeting" is the key to insuring that both aloha and
bonjour respond to this event.

And by watching the chapter-4 namespace, you will see both eventingaloha and
eventingbonjour come to life:

```
$ watch kubectl get pods
NAME                                         READY STATUS  AGE
curler                                       1/1   Running 3m21s
default-broker-filter-c6654bccf-vxm5m        1/1   Running 13m
default-broker-ingress-7479966dc7-pvtx6      1/1   Running 13m
eventingaloha-1-deployment-6cdc888d9d-nlpm8  2/2   Running 6s
eventingbonjour-1-deployment-fc7858b5b-btdcr 2/2   Running 6s
```

You can experiment by using different types of filters in the Subscription to see how the different subscribed services respond. `Filters` may use a CloudEvent attribute for its criteria.

In this chapter, you have learned about Knative Eventing by understanding Event Sources, Event Sinks, and Event Channels; connecting Event Sources to Event Sinks; persisting messages in Event Channels; and filtering messages using Triggers.

In Chapter 6, you will be using filters to categorize events to Sink in and also learn how to enable Knative for observability, which will help you collect metrics and traces for real-world scenarios.

See Also

Knative Documentation on Brokers & Triggers (*https://oreil.ly/ISXPi*)

CHAPTER 5

Observability

Observability, the ability to monitor services and examine traces, is a critically important architectural capability for any event-driven distributed system. Knative leverages Istio (*https://istio.io*) as one of its ingress and gateway implementations. The Istio control plane has the ability to collect the telemetric information. If a few extra components—Prometheus (*https://prometheus.io*), Grafana (*https://grafana.com*), and Jaeger (*https://www.jaegertracing.io*)—are installed in the cluster, then Istio is configured to send the information to them automatically. Thus, observability in Knative can be achieved by simply deploying Prometheus, Grafana, and Jaeger into your Kubernetes cluster.

In this chapter, we will explore how to deploy the observability components, gather the metrics, and explore the traces of Knative-based applications.

Before You Begin

All the recipes in this chapter will be executed from the directory *$BOOK_HOME/ advanced/observability*, so change to the recipe directory by running:

```
$ cd $BOOK_HOME/advanced/observability
```

The recipes in this chapter will deployed in the chapter-5 namespace, so switch to the chapter-5 namespace with the following command:

```
$ kubectl config set-context --current --namespace=chapter-5
```

5.1 Deploying Prometheus and Grafana

Problem

You want to collect and view your Knative Service metrics and analyze them using a dashboard.

Solution

Prometheus is used to collect metrics such as memory and CPU usage from your pods and services. The collected data can then be visualized using Grafana dashboards.

You can deploy Prometheus and Grafana using the script *install-prometheus-grafana.sh*:

```
$ $BOOK_HOME/install/observability/install-prometheus-grafana.sh
```

It will take a few minutes for the components to be installed, and you can monitor the installation progress by watching the pods in the `knative-monitoring` namespace:

```
$ watch kubectl -n knative-monitoring get pods
NAME                                  READY   STATUS    AGE
grafana-5b59764965-nrms9              1/1     Running   84s
kube-state-metrics-5df8bcfdd5-2tksl   1/1     Running   85s
node-exporter-k62nn                   2/2     Running   84s
prometheus-system-0                   1/1     Running   84s
prometheus-system-1                   1/1     Running   84s
```

Discussion

One of the ways to access the Prometheus dashboard is to use Kubernetes NodePort. The Prometheus service by default is accessible only within the cluster; hence, you need to run the following command to expose the Prometheus service using NodePort:

```
$ kubectl expose svc -n knative-monitoring prometheus-system-discovery \
    --type=NodePort --name=prometheus-external
```

Once you have exposed the Prometheus service via NodePort, you can access its dashboard via your web browser using the command:

```
$ minikube svc -n knative-monitoring prometheus-external
```

The command will open the Prometheus dashboard as shown in Figure 5-1 in a new browser window.

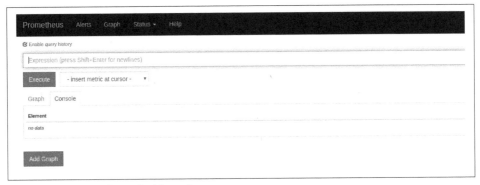

Figure 5-1. Prometheus dashboard

To open the Grafana dashboard you can use the NodePort of the Grafana service. To discover the URL of the service, run the following command:

```
$ minikube service -n knative-monitoring grafana
```

This command will open the Grafana dashboard in your browser, as shown in Figure 5-2.

Figure 5-2. Grafana dashboard

Having successfully installed Prometheus, Knative will not automatically collect and display the telemetry information gathered using Prometheus. The following recipe shows how to configure Knative to allow the use of metrics collected via Prometheus.

5.2 Enable Prometheus for Metrics Collection

Problem

You need to enable the metrics data collection for Knative resources.

Solution

The metrics-related configurations are stored in a ConfigMap called config-observability in the knative-serving namespace. You need to patch the ConfigMap to collect metrics from your Knative pods.

Running the following patch command will update the Knative ConfigMap config-observability to use Prometheus for metrics collection:

```
$ kubectl -n knative-serving patch cm config-observability \
    --patch "$(cat config-observability-patch.yaml)"
```

Discussion

You need to verify if the patch has been successfully applied. To verify, run:

```
$ kubectl -n knative-serving get cm config-observability -oyaml
```

The verification command will show the following YAML output (output trimmed for brevity):

```
1 apiVersion: v1
2 data:
3   metrics.request-metrics-backend-destination: prometheus ❶
4 kind: ConfigMap
5 metadata:
6   name: config-observability
7   namespace: knative-serving
```

❶   Configures Knative to use Prometheus as the backend for metrics

5.3 Installing Jaeger

Problem

You want to capture and review traces through your the Knative Services, to identify slowness and other potential issues.

Solution

Jaeger (*https://www.jaegertracing.io*) can be used to perform end-to-end distributed tracing by propagating x-b3 headers (*https://oreil.ly/9V4nF*) as part of the HTTP requests.

To install Jaeger you should use its Operator (*https://operatorhub.io/operator/jaeger*). We have provided a script that automates the installation of the operator:

```
$ $BOOK_HOME/install/observability/install-jaeger.sh
```

It will take a few minutes for the operator to be installed. You can monitor its progress by watching the pods in the observability namespace:

```
$ watch kubectl -n observability get pods
NAME                            READY   STATUS    AGE
jaeger-operator-7b944bbb5b-gc9kp  1/1     Running   64s
```

Next, deploy the instance of Jaeger with the following script:

```
$ $BOOK_HOME/install/observability/deploy-jaeger.sh
```

Jaeger will be deployed in the istio-system namespace. You can watch the status of the pods in the istio-system namespace with the following command:

```
$ watch kubectl -n istio-system get pods
NAME                                   READY   STATUS    AGE
cluster-local-gateway-777dc6949c-qrn8t   1/1     Running   71m
istio-ingressgateway-6dfbbb4d95-nlw42    1/1     Running   71m
istio-pilot-7bc854755d-s9rxk            1/1     Running   71m
jaeger-54bdd77545-j2v8c                 1/1     Running   15s
```

Discussion

Like Prometheus, the Jaeger service is not exposed outside of the cluster. We need to expose it using the NodePort to be able to access it from the minikube host. Run the following command to expose Jaeger via NodePort:

```
$ kubectl expose svc -n istio-system jaeger-query \
    --type=NodePort --name=jaeger-external
```

Once you have exposed the Jaeger service via NodePort, you can access its dashboard via your web browser using the command:

```
$ minikube service -n istio-system jaeger-external
```

This command will open the Jaeger dashboard as shown in Figure 5-3.

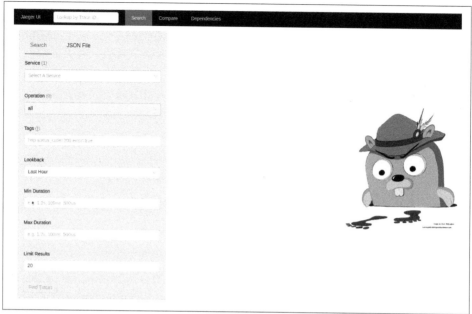

Figure 5-3. Jaeger dashboard

Now that you have your monitoring and tracing services ready to use, it is time to deploy and create load on some Knative Services.

5.4 Deploying Observable Test Services

Problem

You want some microservices that will be monitored and traced.

Solution

In this recipe, you will deploy three Knative Services—customer, preference, and recommendation—and these services will be used in viewing the data collected as part of Knative observability.

Customer is an edge service that is configured to call preference, and preference will call recommendation: customer → preference → recommendation.

The customer service is an always-on service, so its minScale is configured to be 1; on the other hand, the preference service is configured to handle a maximum of 10 concurrent requests only and the recommendation service is left to the default Knative autoscaling configuration:

```
$ kubectl apply -n chapter-5 \
  -f customer.yaml \
  -f preference.yaml \
  -f recommendation.yaml
```

Discussion

It will take a few minutes for the services to be deployed. You can watch the pods in
the chapter-5 namespace:

```
$ watch kubectl get pods
NAME                                                READY  STATUS   AGE
customer-gdrq8-deployment-6cd46d7c7c-mksx9          2/2    Running  6s
preference-g5g7h-deployment-598696f89f-4j4bl        2/2    Running  6s
recommendation-96dxc-deployment-5df6945587-rnqwl    2/2    Running  6s
```

Let's query Knative Serving to see the deployed service URL as shown here:

```
$ watch kubectl -n chapter-5 get ksvc
NAME            URL                                                   READY
customer        http://customer.chapter-5.svc.example.com             True
preference      http://preference.chapter-5.svc.cluster.local         True
recommendation  http://recommendation.chapter-5.svc.cluster.local     True
```

> Try running the PromQL (*https://oreil.ly/IwaNF*): container_mem
> ory_rss   {namespace="chapter-5",container_name="user-
> container"} in the Prometheus dashboard to see how much resi-
> dent set size (RSS)—that is, the nondisk memory such as heap,
> stack etc.—each test application container consumes.

5.5 Customizing the kubectl Output Columns

Problem

You may want to customize the kubectl output columns.

Solution

The output in the previous listing was generated using the kubectl output option
custom columns file (*https://oreil.ly/DINCn*).

To generate the output as shown in the previous listing, create a text file called *csv-
columns.txt* with the following content:

```
NAME           URL          READY ❶
.metadata.name .status.url  .status.conditions[0].status ❷
```

❶ The column headers that will be shown in the output

❷ The values corresponding to each column. The values can be discovered via `kubectl get ksvc <ksvc-name> -o yaml`.

Discussion

In many cases you may want to trim the output columns that are returned by a `kubectl` command. This is useful when you want to look into only a small, specific piece of information from a bigger output.

Let's take an example where you want to view only the Knative Service URL (Knative Route) and its `READY` state from the bigger `kubectl get ksvc` output. In those cases, you can use the *csv-columns.txt* file to trim the output and receive a customized output.

Before viewing the customized output try running `kubectl get ksvc`, observe the output, and then run the following command to appreciate the utility of using custom columns:

```
$ kubectl get ksvc --output=custom-columns-file=csv-columns.txt
```

You should notice that `preference` and `recommendation` have slightly different URLs than `customer`. Recipe 5.6 will explain why.

5.6 Restricting Knative Service Visibility

Problem

You want to restrict service visibility and separate services that are to be consumed outside the cluster versus services that are for internal purposes. In the case of the provided example services, `customer` is the edge service and therefore public, but `preference` and `recommendation` are only for invocation inside the cluster.

Solution

Knative Serving provides the label `serving.knative.dev/visibility` to alert the Knative Serving controller to only create local routes.

Discussion

By default, Knative Services are exposed as public routes; however, the label `serving.knative.dev/visibility` can be applied to the service YAML and results in a `cluster.local` route being generated:

```
apiVersion: serving.knative.dev/v1alpha1
kind: Service
metadata:
```

```
    name: preference
    labels:
      serving.knative.dev/visibility: "cluster-local" ❶
spec:
  template:
    metadata:
      annotations:
        autoscaling.knative.dev/target: "10"
    spec:
      containers:
        - image: quay.io/rhdevelopers/istio-tutorial-preference:v1
          env:
            - name: "COM_REDHAT_DEVELOPER_DEMOS_CUSTOMER_\
                     REST_RECOMMENDATIONSERVICE_MP_REST_URL"
              value: "http://recommendation.knativetutorial.svc.cluster.local"
```

❶ This label will result in a local route for the ksvc: `http://preference.chapter-5.svc.cluster.local`.

When you list your Knative Routes you will see that `preference` and `recommendation` have local routes with the domain name suffix as `chapter-5.svc.cluster.local`, while `customer` has a public address with `example.com` as the domain name suffix:

```
$ kubectl -n chapter-5 get rt
NAME             URL                                                   READY
customer         http://customer.chapter-5.example.com                 True
preference       http://preference.chapter-5.svc.cluster.local         True
recommendation   http://recommendation.chapter-5.svc.cluster.local     True
```

You can call the `customer` service using the script *$BOOK_HOME/bin/call.sh* by passing the parameter `customer`:

```
$ $BOOK_HOME/bin/call.sh customer
customer => preference =>
recommendation v1 from recommendation-96dxc-deployment-5df6945587-rnqwl: 1
```

Grafana Dashboards

The Grafana dashboard provides a list of out-of-the-box dashboards that gather the required metrics across the entire Knative system and its components.

For the next two recipes you will be exploring only two dashboards, as shown in Figure 5-4:

- Knative Serving - Scale Debugging
- Knative Serving - Revision HTTP Requests

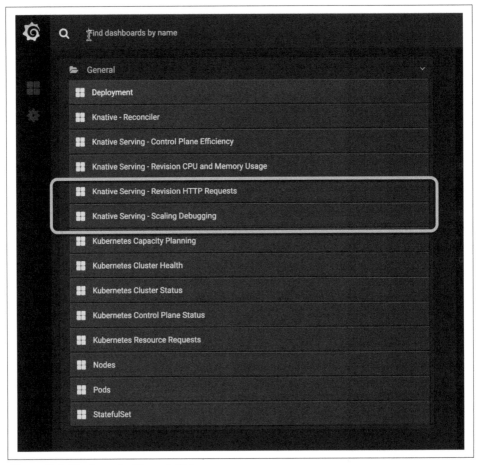

Figure 5-4. Grafana dashboards list

Autoscale Debugging

This dashboard allows you to debug the various aspects of Knative autoscaling, such as:

Revision Pod Counts
 This panel provides the metrics around the Knative Service Revisions and their pod counts: what is actual and what was requested.

Resource Usage
 This panel provides the CPU and memory usage of the Knative Service and its Revisions.

Autoscaler Metrics

This panel provides the metrics around autoscaling of a Knative Service, including data points with respect to a Knative Service's pod counts, concurrency, and Requests Per Second (RPS).

Activator Metrics

This panel shows how the Knative Serving activator is responding to the scale up of dormant Knative Services with details on request count and the time it took to bring the dormant service to life.

5.7 Monitoring Autoscaling Metrics of a Knative Service

Problem

You want to monitor a particular service and find out how it performed during autoscaling.

Solution

The Knative Serving - Scale Debugging dashboard in Grafana provides insight into a particular service's scaling performance.

To simulate the metrics collection, you will run a load test with 50 concurrent requests for a time period of 10 seconds against the `customer` service. As the `prefer ence` service can handle only 10 concurrent requests (`autoscaling.knative.dev/ target: "10"`), you will see that `preference` scales up to handle the extra requests, while `customer` and `recommendation` will be able to handle the load without scaling. Run the load test by calling the script *$BOOK_HOME/bin/load.sh* with the `customer` parameter:

```
$ $BOOK_HOME/bin/load.sh customer
```

Discussion

Analyze the metrics for the `preference` service and discover how it performed during scaling. You can view the Knative Serving - Scale Debugging dashboard by navigating to the Grafana dashboard home and then selecting Home → Knative Serving - Scale Debugging from the list of dashboards.

Figure 5-5 shows the amount of CPU and memory that the `preference` service and its latest revision has consumed. In this case it is approximately `1 CPU` and `500 MB` of memory.

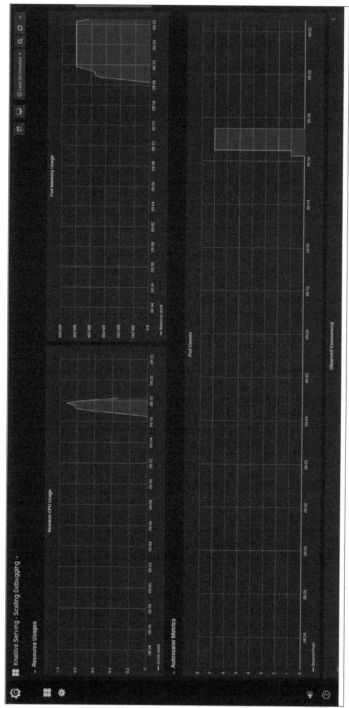

Figure 5-5. Resource usage metrics—Preference (large format version (https://oreil.ly/knative-cookbook-figs))

The screen depicted in Figure 5-6 displays the total number of pods that were used when serving the request along with the observed concurrency. Since target concurrency for the preference service is 10, the pod count will be approximately 6 to 7 pods. The observed concurrency is around 7.

The screen depicted in Figure 5-7 displays similar metrics, such as the actual and requested pod count. Whereas the preference actual pod count tends to be 0 due to the enabled scale-to-zero for the preference service, the requested pod count has spiked close to 7 when handling the load.

The screen depicted in Figure 5-8 displays the number of requests received to activate the preference service distributed by the HTTP response code. It also shows the time that the activator took in responding to the requests. Based on the load that was sent, it shows an average of 50 requests with each taking approximately 9 to 11 seconds to respond.

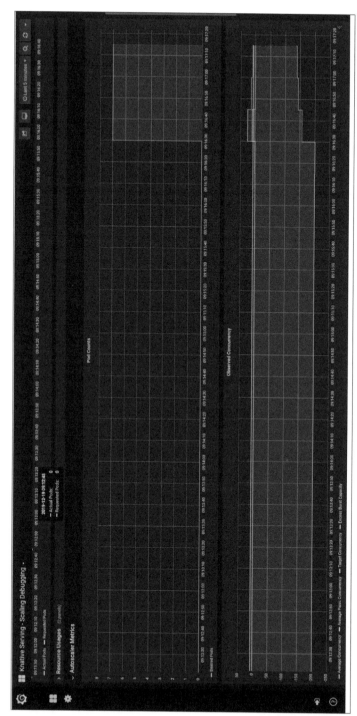

Figure 5-6. Autoscaling metrics—Preference (large format version (https://oreil.ly/knative-cookbook-figs))

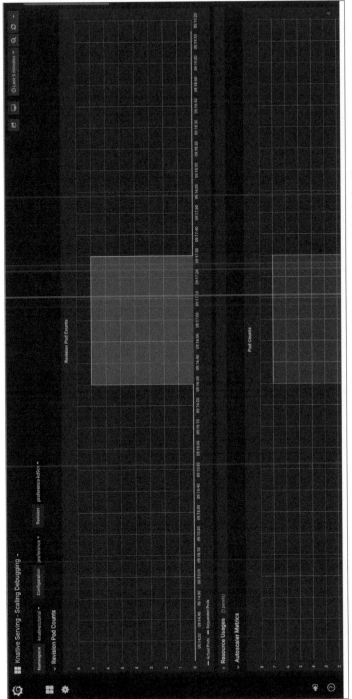

Figure 5-7. Pod counts—Preference (large format version (https://oreil.ly/knative-cookbook-figs))

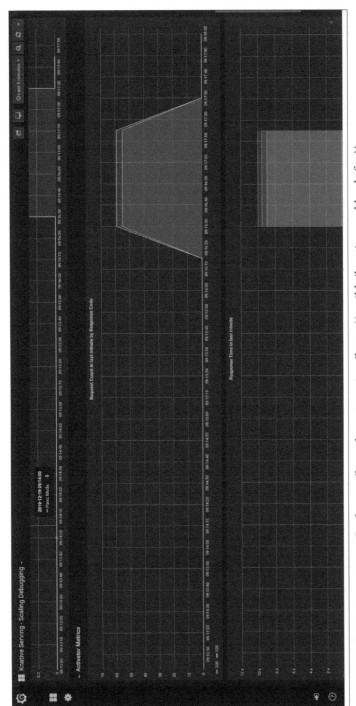

Figure 5-8. Activator metrics—Preference (large format version (https://oreil.ly/knative-cookbook-figs))

5.8 Monitoring HTTP Performance Metrics of a Knative Service

Problem

You want to measure the end-to-end HTTP performance of a Knative Service, such as its request volume, response volume, how many failed requests, how many HTTP 5xx responses, etc.

Solution

The Knative Serving - Revision HTTP Requests dashboard provides metrics for each Knative Service Revision's HTTP requests. This dashboard has three panels:

Overview
> This panel provides HTTP request and response overview with metrics around Operations per second (Ops) and responses based on the HTTP response code.

Request Volume
> This panel provides HTTP request-centric metrics with request volumes classified by revision and response codes for each Knative Service and its Revision.

Response Volume
> This panel provides HTTP response-centric data with response volumes by response time and response code for each Knative Service and its Revisions.

Discussion

As `customer` is an edge service, it will be the ideal service for you to monitor the end-to-end request and response metrics.

Select "Knative Serving - Revision HTTP Requests" from the list of dashboards in Grafana home. You will see a screen similar to the one depicted in Figure 5-9, which has an overview of the `customer` service requests and responses. It also provides the metrics around requests alone categorized on request volume by revision and HTTP response codes.

The request volume–based metrics, e.g., Operations per second (Ops), will have only one revision of the `customer` service deployed with its average Ops being approximately 1.7. The response code-based metrics are predominantly HTTP 200 with some HTTP 5xx in the response code, which happened when the service was in a dormant state and the Knative activator was trying to scale it up.

With the dashboard depicted in Figure 5-10 you will observe percentile distribution of the `customer` service responses by revision and HTTP response codes.

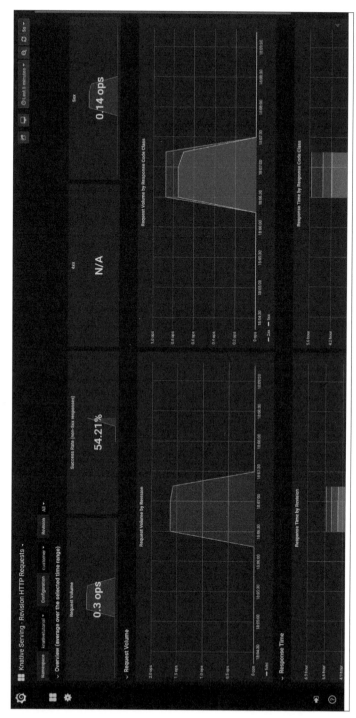

Figure 5-9. Request Volume metrics—Customer (large format version (https://oreil.ly/knative-cookbook-figs))

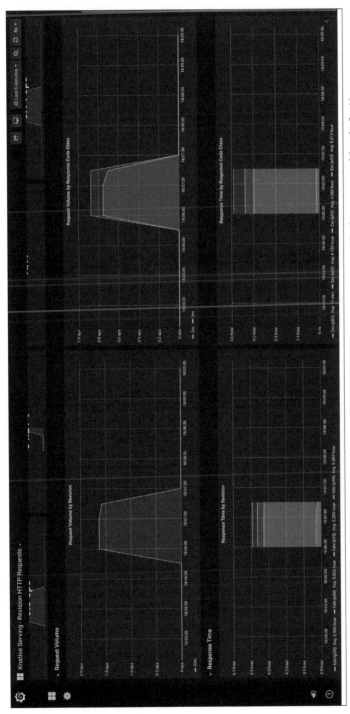

Figure 5-10. Response Volume metrics—Customer (large format version (https://oreil.ly/knative-cookbook-figs))

5.9 Tracing Knative Services with Jaeger

Problem

You want to trace the end-to-end call through a series of Knative Services.

For example: customer → preference → recommendation.

Solution

The Istio `istio-ingressgateway` automatically adds the `x-b3` headers for all the HTTP requests that pass through it. With the installation and enablement of the Jaeger component, the Knative Services will generate the trace spans automatically and those spans can then be viewed in the Jaeger dashboard.

Discussion

For better clarity, it is good to clean up the existing Jaeger traces generated by previous load test runs. A simple solution to getting back to a known clean state is to simply delete the Jaeger pod in `istio-system` and let a new pod spin up as Jaeger stores its cached data in-memory.

You can run the following command to delete the Jaeger pod:

```
$ JAEGER_POD=$(kubectl -n istio-system get pod \
 -l "app.kubernetes.io/name=jaeger" -o jsonpath={.items[0].metadata.name})
$ kubectl -n istio-system delete pod $JAEGER_POD
```

It may take a few seconds for the Jaeger pod to come back to life. You can watch the status of pods in the `istio-system` namespace to monitor its lifecycle.

Make sure that `kubectl proxy` is still running and open the Jaeger dashboard (*https://oreil.ly/pdASw*) in your web browser.

Run a single call to the `customer` service using the script *$BOOK_HOME/bin/call.sh* but passing the parameter `customer` to it. The call should return you a response like `customer` ⇒ `preference` ⇒ `recommendation` `v1` from `recommendation-96dxc-deployment-5df6945587-rnqwl: 1`.

Use the browser refresh button to refresh the Jaeger dashboard to have the `customer` service listed in the Service drop-down, as shown in Figure 5-11.

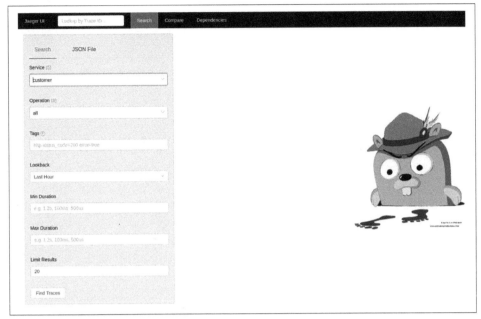

Figure 5-11. Jaeger service list

Leaving all the other search options with their defaults, click the Find Traces button where you will see one trace with eight spans as shown in Figure 5-12.

Clicking the `customer` span as depicted in Figure 5-11 will the expand the trace to show the end-to-end details, as shown in Figure 5-12.

You should notice that the initial call to the Knative Service is routed via `istio-ingressgateway`, which then:

1. Forwards the call to the `customer` Knative Service

2. The `customer` service then calls `preference` via the `cluster-local-gateway`

3. Finally, the `preference` service calls `recommendation` also via `cluster-local-gateway`

Based on the service flow as described earlier, Jaeger provides a critical data point as shown in Figure 5-13; the traces that show the time spent on each service hop. With these details, you can discover how transactions are flowing through your system as well as determine if there are any bottlenecks along the path.

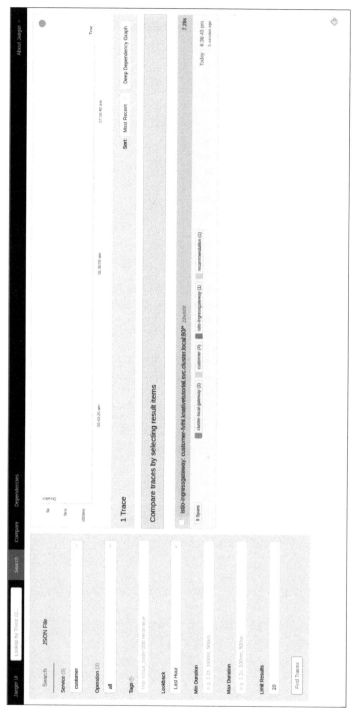

Figure 5-12. Jaeger customer trace (large format version (https://oreilly/knative-cookbook-figs))

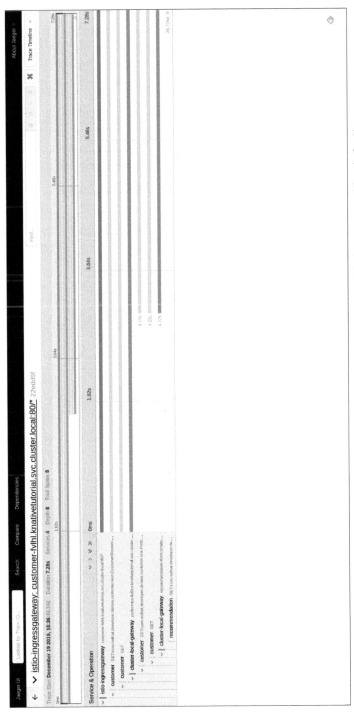

Figure 5-13. Jaeger customer trace expanded (large format version (https://oreil.ly/knative-cookbook-figs))

The exploration of logging requires a bigger cluster with more CPU and memory than the simple minikube configuration used in these recipes. If you have access to a bigger cluster, you should also review the logging capabilities following the upstream project documentation (*https://oreil.ly/CMyUN*).

You now have a good understanding of configuring metrics and monitoring collection using Prometheus, analyzing the metrics via the Grafana dashboard, and identifying the bottlenecks of your services using the Jaeger trace spans. In the next chapter, you will learn how to apply Enterprise Integration Patterns using Knative and Apache Camel-K.

CHAPTER 6

Serverless Integration Patterns Using Apache Camel-K

It is highly recommended that you have reviewed and completed the recipes from Chapters 3 and 4 of the cookbook before reading this chapter.

The recipes in this chapter will assume that you are fluent in those concepts and that you have properly installed those prerequisites.

Within the average large IT organization, it is very rare that you would ever build a new application that would live in total isolation, one that would be completely detached from all other old or new systems. Many real-time use cases demand that the old and new systems share and exchange data.

Apache Camel (*https://camel.apache.org*) is an open source framework that helps you integrate systems. Apache Camel allows the integrated systems to produce and consume data between them. It provides over 300 components that include integration connectors (*https://oreil.ly/2oTmP*) to sources such as TCP, ActiveMQ, FTP, and Salesforce.com, which makes it easier to integrate heterogeneous systems. Enterprise Integration Patterns (EIP) (*https://www.enterpriseintegrationpatterns.com*) provide solutions to many common integration problems. Apache Camel provides implementations of these patterns via its rich Domain Specific Language (DSL) (*https://oreil.ly/jEBcN*), thereby making it easier for the developers to apply the EIP easily.

Apache Camel-K (*https://oreil.ly/RPuj-*) aims at simplifying the programming and deployment model for Apache Camel integrations. By working with Apache Camel-K, the integration developers can now focus on writing their integrations using the Camel DSL in Java, JavaScript, Groovy, XML or YAML, without the need to worry about how to package and deploy them.

Camel-K will enable you to craft a Kubernetes-native integration application. It also leverages serverless capabilities via Knative.

Before You Begin

All the recipes in this chapter will be executed from the directory $BOOK_HOME/ advanced/camel-k, so change to the recipe directory by running:

```
$ cd $BOOK_HOME/advanced/camel-k
```

The recipes of this chapter will be deployed in the namespace chapter-6. You need switch to the chapter-6 namespace:

```
$ kubectl config set-context --current --namespace=chapter-6
```

6.1 Installing Camel-K

Problem

You want to install Apache Camel-K in your Kubernetes cluster.

Solution

Download correct the kamel (*https://oreil.ly/o_GDr*) release for your operating system, extract the binary, and add it to your $PATH. As of the writing of this book, the version of kamel was 1.0.0-RC2; run the following command to verify if are using version 1.0.0-RC2 or above:

```
$ kamel version
Camel K Client 1.0.0-RC2
```

 The command-line tool is called kamel while the technology itself is called Camel-K.

To install Camel-K in your cluster, run the command kamel install --wait:

```
$ kamel install --wait
platform "camel-k" in phase Creating
platform "camel-k" in phase Ready
Camel K installed in namespace chapter-6
```

Discussion

As with other installations in this book, this process will take a few minutes for the Camel-K pods to be up and running. You can monitor the progress of the installation by watching the pods in the `chapter-6` namespace:

```
$ watch kubectl -n chapter-6 get pods
NAME                                   READY   STATUS    RESTARTS   AGE
camel-k-operator-84d7896b68-9mfdv      1/1     Running   0          2m7s
```

The primary responsibility of `camel-k-operator` is to look for Camel-K integrations that are deployed using `kamel`, and to build and deploy them as Kubernetes applications. The Camel-K install creates a ConfigMap called `camel-k-maven-settings`, which will be used by the Camel-K integrations to download the Apache Camel Maven artifacts. The next recipe will show you how to modify the Camel-K Maven settings ConfigMap called `camel-k-maven-settings` to make the integration builds run faster.

6.2 Configuring Camel-K to Build Faster

Problem

You want to make your Camel-K builds and deployments faster.

Solution

Camel-K uses Apache Maven (*https://maven.apache.org*) to build the integration kits and Camel-K's related containers. The Apache Maven settings for Camel-K are stored in a ConfigMap called `camel-k-maven-settings` in the `chapter-6` namespace. One of the ways to make the build faster is by using a Maven repository manager such as Sonatype Nexus (*https://oreil.ly/-q1l-*), which helps in caching the Maven artifacts from remote repositories and serves them from local repositories the subsequent times they are asked to be downloaded.

Edit the ConfigMap using the command:

```
$ kubectl edit cm camel-k-maven-settings
```

This command by default opens the ConfigMap YAML in vi, a text editor. We can use the environment variable `KUBE_EDITOR` to allow us to edit the YAML with the editor of our choice. For example, setting `export KUBE_EDITOR=code -w` will make the `kubectl edit` commands to open the Kubernetes resource YAML in VSCode (*https://code.visualstudio.com*).

Discussion

The following listing shows the Camel-K maven settings configured to use a Sonatype Nexus repository as its mirror:

```
apiVersion: v1
data:
  settings.xml: |-
    <?xml version="1.0" encoding="UTF-8"?>
    <settings xmlns="http://maven.apache.org/SETTINGS/1.0.0"
xmlns:xsi="http://www.w3.org/2001/XMLSchema-instance"
xsi:schemaLocation="http://maven.apache.org/SETTINGS/1.0.0
https://maven.apache.org/xsd/settings-1.0.0.xsd">
        <localRepository></localRepository>
        <mirrors>
          <mirror>
            <id>central</id>
            <name>central</name>
            <url>http://nexus:8081/nexus/content/groups/public</url> ❶
            <mirrorOf>*</mirrorOf>
          </mirror>
        </mirrors>
        ...
    </settings>
kind: ConfigMap
metadata:
  labels:
    app: camel-k
  name: camel-k-maven-settings
  namespace: chapter-6
```

❶ This repository address needs to be updated as per your cluster setting. In this example, the Sonatype Nexus repository manager is installed in the chapter-6 namespace.

 If you don't have a Sonatype Nexus repository, you can deploy one into the cluster using the deployment *$BOOK_HOME/apps/nexus/app.yaml*.

6.3 Writing a Camel-K Integration

Problem

You want to write a very simple integration with Camel-K.

Solution

An integration is an Apache Camel route defined using Camel DSL. The `kamel` CLI will help you build and run the Apache Camel integration as a Kubernetes application. The Camel-K Kubernetes operator takes care of performing the necessary background tasks such as converting the Camel DSL to Java, downloading the required Maven artifacts, building the application, and finally, using those built artifacts to then build a Linux container image.

In this recipe you will deploy a simple microservice that prints out the text "Welcome to Camel K" every 10 seconds. If you have worked with Apache Camel before, you may be familiar with using the Apache Camel DSL with Java and XML, but in this chapter you will be using the Apache Camel DSL in YAML.

The Apache Camel YAML DSL is still under active development, but using this DSL will give you a consistent resource definition across Kubernetes, Knative, and Camel-K.

Let's analyze your first Camel-K integration before running it. A Camel-K integration resource is an array of one flow or multiple route definitions. The following listing shows you a simple timer integration with just one route:

```
- from:
    uri: "timer:tick"  ❶
    parameters:  ❷
      period: "10s"
    steps:  ❸
      - set-body:  ❹
          constant: "Welcome to Apache Camel K"
      - set-header:  ❺
          name: ContentType
          simple: text/plain
      - transform:  ❻
          simple: "${body.toUpperCase()}"
      - to:  ❼
          uri: "log:info?multiline=true&showAll=true"
```

❶ The Apache Camel producer Uniform Resource Identifier (URI), which in this case is the timer (*https://oreil.ly/gQjS4*) component.

❷ `parameters` allows you to specify the configurable properties of the component. In this case the timer component needs to tick every 10 seconds.

❸ `steps` defines the flow of your Camel exchange (IN). Each Camel-K integration should have at least one step defined.

❹ Sets the body of the Camel exchange (OUT), a constant value of "Welcome to Apache Camel K."

❺ You can also set headers as part of the step. This sets the `ContentType` header with the value `text/plain`.

❻ You can also apply transformations as part of a step. This applies a simple transformation of converting the exchange OUT body to uppercase.

❼ In the end you send the processed exchange (OUT) to its desired destination; here we simply log it out.

You can have any number of steps as needed for an integration based on your use case. In later sections of this chapter you will deploy multistep-based integration examples.

Navigate to *$BOOK_HOME/advanced/camel-k* and then run the following command to deploy your first Camel-K integration:

```
$ kamel run --dev --dependency camel:log get-started/timed-greeter.yaml
integration "timed-greeter" created
integration "timed-greeter" in phase Initialization
integration "timed-greeter" in phase Building Kit
integration "timed-greeter" in phase Deploying
integration "timed-greeter" in phase Running
...
```

Discussion

You need to use the `kamel` CLI to deploy a Camel-K integration. The command starts the Camel-K integration in development mode with the option `--dev`. The development mode adds the option to tail the logs from the integration's Kubernetes pod and adds support to synchronize the source changes and reload the Apache Camel context automatically.

Since Apache Camel 3, the entire Apache Camel platform has been modularized, and the core module does not have all the components that are needed for this integration. You can instruct the Camel-K integration to add extra Camel component modules (JARs) that you need via the `--dependency` parameter. In this case you are adding the `camel:log` component as part of your integration deployment.

A typical Camel-K integration deployment will take approximately 2–5 minutes, as it involves multiple steps, including:

1. Building an integration kit (`camel-k-kit`), which builds the container image with all the required Camel modules downloaded and added to the classpath within the container image.

2. If using Knative, then deploy as a Knative Service.

3. Run the container image as a Kubernetes pod and start the Camel context.

```
$ watch kubectl -n chapter-6 get pods
NAME                                         READY   STATUS      RESTARTS   AGE
camel-k-kit-bnvcv2t88vdk4ri5mdd0             0/1     Completed   0          6m2s
camel-k-kit-bnvcv2t88vdk4ri5mdd0-builder     0/1     Completed   0          6m11s
timed-greeter-cd8b58cdb-dn75q                1/1     Running     0          26s
```

In the same terminal as the `kamel run`, you will see the output logging of the Camel-K integration as shown here:

```
$ kamel run --dev --dependency camel:log get-started/timed-greeter.yaml
...
[1] 2020-01-13 03:25:28.548 INFO  [Camel (camel-k) thread #1 - timer://tick]
info - Exchange[
[1]    Id: ID-timed-greeter-57b4d49974-vg859-1578885868551-0-13
[1]    ExchangePattern: InOnly
[1]    Properties: {CamelCreatedTimestamp=Mon Jan 13 03:25:28 UTC 2020,
CamelExternalRedelivered=false, CamelMessageHistory=[DefaultMessageHistory
[routeId=route1, node=setBody1], DefaultMessageHistory[routeId=route1,
node=setHeader1], DefaultMessageHistory[routeId=route1, node=transform1],
DefaultMessageHistory[routeId=route1, node=to1]], CamelTimerCounter=7,
CamelTimerFiredTime=Mon Jan 13 03:25:28 UTC 2020, CamelTimerName=tick,
CamelTimerPeriod=10000, CamelToEndpoint=log://info?multiline=true&showAll=true}
[1]    Headers: {ContentType=text/plain, firedTime=Mon Jan 13 03:25:28 UTC 2020}
[1]    BodyType: String
[1]    Body: WELCOME TO APACHE CAMEL K
[1] ]
```

Update the *timed-greeter.yaml* body text to be "Hi Camel K rocks!" and observe the automatic reloading of the context and the logs printing the new message.

If you are not using the Maven repository manager or it takes a long time to download Maven artifacts, your earlier command `kamel run --dev ..` will report a failure. In those cases, run the command `kamel get` to see the status of the integration.

Once you see the `timed-greeter` pod running, use `kamel log timed-greeter` to see the logs as shown in the earlier listing.

You can use Ctrl-C to stop the running Camel-K integration and automatically terminate its pods. If you encountered the dev mode failure as described earlier, try to delete the integration using the command `kamel delete timed-greeter`.

6.4 Running Camel-K Integrations as Knative Serverless Services

Problem

You want to run a Camel-K integration as a serverless service.

Solution

Any Camel-K integration can be converted into a serverless service using Knative. For an integration to be deployed as a Knative Service, you need to use Camel-K's Knative component.

The Camel-K Knative component provides two consumers: `knative:endpoint` and `knative:channel`. The former is used to deploy the integration as a Knative Service, while the latter is used to handle events from a Knative Event Channel.

> The Knative endpoints can be either a Camel producer or consumer depending on the context and need.

In this recipe you will deploy a `knative:endpoint` consumer as part of your integration, which will add the serverless capabilities to your Camel-K integration using Knative.

The following listing shows a simple echoer Knative Camel-K integration that will simply respond to your Knative Service call with the same body that you sent into it in uppercase form. If there is no body received, the service will respond with "no body received":

```
- from:
    uri: "knative:endpoint/echoer" ❶
    steps:
      - log:
          message: "Got Message: ${body}"
      - convert-body: "java.lang.String" ❷
      - choice:
```

```
when:
  - simple: "${body} != null && ${body.length} > 0"
    steps:
      - set-body:
          simple: "${body.toUpperCase()}"
      - set-header:
          name: ContentType
          simple: text/plain
      - log:
          message: "${body}"
otherwise:
  steps:
    - set-body:
        constant: "no body received"
    - set-header:
        name: ContentType
        simple: text/plain
    - log:
        message: "Otherwise::${body}"
```

❶ The consumer needs to be a Knative endpoint URI of the form knative:end point/<*your endpoint name*>. The name of the Knative Service will be the last path segment of the URI; in this case, your Knative Service will be called echoer.

❷ You will be converting the incoming data (request body) to java.lang.String as that will help you in converting to uppercase.

You can run this integration as shown in the following snippet. Notice that you are now deploying the integration in production mode; i.e., without the --dev option:

```
$ kamel run --wait --dependency camel:log --dependency camel:bean \
    get-started/echoer.yaml
```

 You can use stern camel-k to monitor the progress of the builder pod, as well as watch kubectl kamel get and monitor the PHASE column. In addition, watch kubectl get ksvc checks for the READY column to become True.

Since the production mode takes some time for the integration to come up, you need to watch the integration's logs using the command kamel log <*integration name*> in this case, kamel log echoer, and you can get the name of the integration using the command kamel get.

Discussion

In the integration that you deployed, you applied the Choice EIP when processing the exchange body. When the body has content, it simply converts the body to upper-case; otherwise, it returns a canned response of "no body received." In either case, the content type header is set to text/plain.

Camel-K defines an integration via Custom Resource Definitions (CRDs), and you can view those CRDs and the actual integrations via the following commands:

```
$ kubectl api-resources --api-group=camel.apache.org
NAME                  SHORTNAMES APIGROUP          NAMESPACED KIND
builds                           camel.apache.org  true       Build
camelcatalogs         cc         camel.apache.org  true       CamelCatalog
integrationkits       ik         camel.apache.org  true       IntegrationKit
integrationplatforms  ip         camel.apache.org  true       IntegrationPlatform
integrations          it         camel.apache.org  true       Integration

$ watch kubectl -n chapter-6 get integrations
NAME         PHASE     KIT                         REPLICAS
echoer       Running   kit-bodug9d83u4bmr3uh8jg    1
```

Once the integration is started, you can check the Knative Service using the command kubectl -n chapter-6 get ksvc echoer.

When the service is in a ready state use the call script *$BOOK_HOME/bin/call.sh* with the parameter echoer and a request body of "Hello World":

```
$ $BOOK_HOME/bin/call.sh echoer 'Hello World'
HELLO WORLD

$ $BOOK_HOME/bin/call.sh echoer ''
no body received
```

The invocation of a Knative Camel-K integration is a bit different than previous Knative test calls. The Knative Camel-K integration service is expecting a POST where the input data is part of the request body. Therefore, you need a few different elements to construct the invocation. The following snippet from *$BOOK_HOME/bin/call.sh* shows how a Knative Service call is constructed:

```
$ NODE_PORT=$(kubectl get svc istio-ingressgateway -n istio-system \
-o jsonpath={.spec.ports[?(@.port==80)].nodePort}) ❶
$ IP_ADDRESS="$(minikube ip):$NODE_PORT" ❷
$ HOST_HEADER="Host:echoer.chapter-6.example.com" ❸
$ curl -X POST -H $HOST_HEADER -d "Hello World" $IP_ADDRESS ❹
```

❶ All Knative traffic should flow through the Istio ingress gateway, and NodePort is the easiest solution on minikube.

❷ Minikube, which is running as a VM on your local machine, provides a local IP address (e.g., 192.168.99.100).

❸ The host header can be determined by running kubectl get ksvc echoer. Just make sure to remove the "http://" prefix.

❹ curl with a POST.

 Explore the kamel tool via its help option kamel --help to see the list of available commands and their respective options.

6.5 Using Knative Eventing with Camel-K

Problem

You want to leverage Camel-K integration capabilities within Knative Eventing by deploying the CamelSource event source.

Solution

The CamelSource event source allows you use a Camel-K integration as part of the Knative Eventing architecture. Simply speaking, you can make the Camel-K integration act as a Knative Event Source (*https://oreil.ly/nzre1*) and send the Camel exchanges (OUT) through a Knative Event Sink.

Discussion

The CamelSource event source does not come with the default Knative Eventing installation; therefore, you need to install it from the Knative Eventing contribution repository (*https://oreil.ly/0QAT_*).

The following snippet depicts how to deploy the CamelSource into the knative-sources namespace:

```
$ kubectl apply \
  -f "https://github.com/knative/eventing-contrib/releases/\
download/v0.12.2/camel.yaml"
```

You will see a new pod showing up the knative-sources namespace:

```
$ watch kubectl -n knative-sources get pods
NAME                         READY   STATUS    RESTARTS   AGE
camel-controller-manager-0   1/1     Running   0          12h
```

In addition, CamelSource is now part of the API for your Kubernetes cluster:

```
$ kubectl api-resources --api-group=sources.eventing.knative.dev
NAME               APIGROUP                       NAMESPACED   KIND
apiserversources   sources.eventing.knative.dev   true         ApiServerSource
camelsources       sources.eventing.knative.dev   true         CamelSource
containersources   sources.eventing.knative.dev   true         ContainerSource
```

```
cronjobsources      sources.eventing.knative.dev    true      CronJobSource
sinkbindings        sources.eventing.knative.dev    true      SinkBinding
kafkasources        sources.eventing.knative.dev    true      KafkaSource
```

6.6 Logging and Displaying CloudEvents Messages

Problem

You want to watch the raw CloudEvents (CE) messages that are exchanged between Knative Eventing Channels and Subscribers.

Solution

In order for you to view the events drained from the `CamelSource` `timed-greeter`, you need to deploy a utility service called `event-display`. Run the following command to deploy the service:

```
$ kubectl apply \
  -f "https://github.com/knative/eventing-contrib/releases/\
download/v0.12.0/event-display.yaml"

$ watch "kubectl -n chapter-6 get pods \
  -l serving.knative.dev/service=event-display"
NAME              URL                                          READY
event-display     http://event-display.chapter-6.example.com   True
```

Discussion

The `event-display` is a Knative Service, which when configured as an event sink will simply log the raw CloudEvents (*https://cloudevents.io*) generated from its Knative Event Source. In the case of `timed-greeter`, all the events—i.e., the message "Welcome to Apache Camel-K" from the `timed-greeter` `CamelSource`—will be sent to the `event-display` service.

6.7 Wiring a CamelSource to a Knative Eventing Sink

Problem

You want to drain the output of a Camel exchange to a Knative Eventing Sink.

Solution

Knative Eventing semantics allows you to link the Event Source to the Event Sink using the `sink` block of the Knative Eventing source specification.

As part of this recipe you will deploy the same `timed-greeter` integration that you deployed earlier, but this time as a `CamelSource`. The event source (`CamelSource`) is configured to drain the events to the sink `event-display`. The following listing provides the details of `CamelSource` configuration:

```
apiVersion: sources.eventing.knative.dev/v1alpha1 ❶
kind: CamelSource
metadata:
  name: timed-greeter
spec:
  integration: ❷
    dependencies:
      - camel:log
  source: ❸
    flow:
      from:
        uri: "timer:tick"
        parameters:
          period: "10s"
        steps:
          - set-body:
              constant: "Welcome to Apache Camel-K"
          - set-header:
              name: ContentType
              simple: text/plain
          - transform:
              simple: "${body.toUpperCase()}"
          - log:
              message: "${body}"
  sink: ❹
    ref:
      apiVersion: serving.knative.dev/v1
      kind: Service
      name: event-display
```

❶ The `CamelSource` is provided by the API `sources.eventing.knative.dev`. It is now available as a result of deploying the `CamelSource` event source.

❷ The `CamelSource` spec has two main sections: `integration` and `source`. The `integration` block is used to configure the Camel-K integration–specific properties such as dependencies, traits, etc. In this example we add the required dependencies such as `camel:log`, which is the dependency that you passed earlier via the `kamel` CLI.

❸ The `source` block is used to define the Camel-K integration definition. The `flow` attribute of the `source` block allows you define the Camel route.

❹ The event sink for messages from the Camel event source. The sink could be either a Knative Service, Knative Event Channel, or Knative Event Broker. In this case it is configured to be the `event-display` Knative Service.

Discussion

You can deploy the `CamelSource` in the same way you deploy any other Kubernetes resource. The following listing shows you how:

```
$ kubectl apply -n chapter-6 -f get-started/timed-greeter-source.yaml
camelsource.sources.eventing.knative.dev/timed-greeter created
```

It will take a few minutes for the `CamelSource` to be reconciled and start to emit greeter events. You can watch the `chapter-6` pods to monitor the status of the deployment.

A successful deployment will show the `CamelSource` `timed-greeter` in the ready state along with its pods in the `chapter-6` namespace. You will also see the `event-display` pod scaling up to receive the events from `timed-greeter`:

```
$ watch kubectl -n chapter-6 get camelsources
NAME             READY    AGE
timed-greeter    True     114s

$ watch kubectl -n chapter-6 get pods
NAME                                              READY    STATUS    AGE
camel-k-operator-84d7896b68-sgmpk                 1/1      Running   2m36s
event-display-dmq4s-deployment-775789b565-fnf2t   2/2      Running   17s
timed-greeter-m4chq-7cbf4ddc66-kxpqd              1/1      Running   86s
```

Open a new terminal and run the following command to start watching the events that are being drained into the `event-display` Knative Service using the command `stern -n chapter-6 event-display -c user-container`:

```
$ stern -n chapter-6 event-display -c user-container
event-... user-container    id: ID-timed-greeter-m4chq-7cbf4ddc66-kxpqd-1577072133
461-0-19
event-... user-container    time: 2019-12-23T03:37:03.432Z
event-... user-container Data,
event-... user-container    WELCOME TO APACHE CAMEL K
event-... user-container ☁  cloudevents.Event
event-... user-container Validation: valid
event-... user-container Context Attributes,
event-... user-container    specversion: 0.3
event-... user-container    type: org.apache.camel.event
event-... user-container    source: camel-source:knativetutorial/timed-greeter
```

Once you have verified the output, you can delete the `CamelSource` using the command:

```
$ kubectl -n chapter-6 delete camelsource timed-greeter
```

After a few seconds you will see the `event-display` Knative Service scaling down to zero since it no longer receives events via the event source.

6.8 Applying Enterprise Integration Patterns with Camel-K

Problem

You want to poll a public REST API, push the data into an Apache Kafka Topic, and based on the message contents, route particular messages of interest out to an awaiting browser window.

Solution

In this recipe you will be applying the pattern called Content Based Router (*https://oreil.ly/vBXOi*) and will combine several of the recipes in this cookbook into a single cohesive application.

Apache Camel supports numerous Enterprise Integration Patterns (EIPs) out-of-the-box (*https://oreil.ly/B2w4O*).

Content Based Router

The Content Based Router examines the message content and routes the message to a different channel based on the data contained in the message. The routing can be based on a number of criteria, such as existence of fields, specific field values, etc. When implementing a Content Based Router, special caution should be taken to make the routing function easy to maintain as the router can become a point of frequent maintenance. In more sophisticated integration scenarios, the Content Based Router can take on the form of a configurable rules engine that computes the destination channel based on a set of configurable rules.

This recipe involves a simple data-streaming application that will use Camel-K and Knative to process the incoming data, where that processed data is pushed out to a reactive web application via Server-Sent Events (SSE) (*https://oreil.ly/PTARb*) as shown in Figure 6-1.

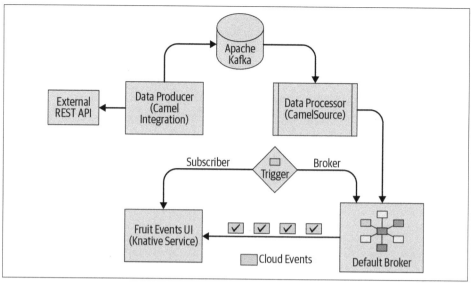

Figure 6-1. Application overview

As you see in Figure 6-1, the application has the following components:

Data Producer
> The Camel-K integration application that will produce data simulating the streaming data by sending the data to Apache Kafka

Data Processor
> The Camel-K integration application that will process the streaming data from Kafka and send the default Knative Eventing Broker

Event Subscriber (Fruits UI)
> The Quarkus (*https://quarkus.io*) Java application that will display the processed data from the Data Processor

Event Trigger
> The Knative Event Trigger (Recipe 4.10) that applies a filter on the processed data to send to the Event Subscriber

The upcoming recipes will deploy these individual components, and then we will test the integration by wiring them all together.

Discussion

Now would be a good time to review Chapter 4. Before you start to deploy the elements of this recipe, you need to verify the following prerequisites:

1. Apache Kafka `my-cluster` (Recipe 4.6) is running in the `kafka` namespace. You can verify the Kafka cluster using the command `kubectl get kafkas -n kafka`. The creation of `my-cluster` was described in Chapter 4.

2. The `chapter-6` namespace is labeled to inject Knative Eventing's default Broker filter and ingress deployment:

    ```
    $ kubectl label namespace chapter-6 knative-eventing-injection=enabled
    ```

    If the label is set correctly on the `chapter-6` namespace, you should see the following pods corresponding to Knative Eventing's default Broker's filter and ingress:

    ```
    $ watch kubectl get pods -n chapter-6
    NAME                                       READY   STATUS    AGE
    camel-k-operator-5d74595cdf-4v9qz          1/1     Running   3h59m
    default-broker-filter-c6654bccf-zkw7s      1/1     Running   59s
    default-broker-ingress-857698bc5b-r4zmf    1/1     Running   59s
    ```

6.9 Deploying a Data Producer

Problem

You want an application that could act as a *streaming data producer*.

Solution

In this recipe we will deploy a Knative Camel-K integration called `fruits-producer`, which will use a public fruits API (*http://fruityvice.com*) to retrieve information about fruits and stream the data to Apache Kafka. The `fruits-producer` service retrieves the data from the fruits API, splits it using the Split EIP (*https://oreil.ly/9CyMg*), and then sends the data to a Kafka Topic called `fruits`.

The following command deploys the `fruits-producer` Knative Service:

```
- from:
    uri: "knative:endpoint/fruits-producer"
    steps:
      - set-header:
          name: CamelHttpMethod
          constant: GET
      - to: "http:fruityvice.com/api/fruit/all?bridgeEndpoint=true"  ❶
      - split:
          jsonpath: "$.[*]"  ❷
```

```
- marshal:
    json: {}
- log:
    message: "${body}"
- to: "kafka:fruits?brokers=my-cluster-kafka-bootstrap.kafka:9092" ❸
```

❶ Call the external REST API *http://fruityvice.com* to get the list of fruits to simulate the data streaming

❷ Apply the Camel Split EIP to split the JSON array to individual records

❸ Send the processed data—i.e., the individual fruit record—as JSON to the Apache Kafka Topic:

```
$ kamel -n chapter-6 run \
 --wait \
 --dependency camel:log \
 --dependency camel:jackson \
 --dependency camel:jsonpath \
 eip/fruits-producer.yaml
integration "fruits-producer" created
integration "fruits-producer" in phase Initialization
integration "fruits-producer" in phase Building Kit
```

The service deployment may take several minutes to become available. To monitor the status, run one of the following:

- watch kubectl get pods
- watch kamel get
- watch kubectl get ksvc

```
$ watch kubectl -n chapter-6 get pods --field-selector=status.phase=Running
NAME                                              READY  STATUS   AGE
camel-k-operator-5d74595cdf-4v9qz                 1/1    Running  4h4m
default-broker-filter-c6654bccf-zkw7s             1/1    Running  5m
default-broker-ingress-857698bc5b-r4zmf           1/1    Running  5m
fruits-producer-nfngm-deployment-759c797c44-d6r52 2/2    Running  70s

$ kubectl -n chapter-6 get ksvc
NAME             URL                                            READY
event-display    http://event-display.chapter-6.example.com     True
fruits-producer  http://fruits-producer.chapter-6.example.com   True
```

Discussion

You can verify if `fruits-producer` is working by calling the Knative Service using the script *$BOOK_HOME/bin/call.sh* with the parameter `fruits-producer`. To check if the data has been received in the Kafka Topic, open a new terminal and execute the script *$BOOK_HOME/bin/kafka-consumer.sh* with the parameter `fruits`. If Camel-K integration has sent the data correctly, you should see few fruits listed in the JSON data in the Kafka consumer console:

```
$ $BOOK_HOME/bin/call.sh fruits-producer ''
```

```
$ $BOOK_HOME/bin/kafka-consumer.sh fruits
...
{"genus":"Citrullus","name":"Watermelon","id":25,"family":"Cucurbitaceae",
"order":"Cucurbitales","nutritions":{"carbohydrates":8,"protein":0.6,"fat":0.2,
"calories":30,"sugar":6}}
```

 Since the fruits API returns a static set of fruit data consistently, you can call it as needed to simulate data streaming and it will always be the same data.

6.10 Deploying a Data Processor

Problem

You need an integration application—i.e., a *data processor*—that can process the streaming data from Apache Kafka.

Solution

In this recipe you will deploy a `CamelSource` called `fruits-processor` that can handle and process the streaming data from the Kafka Topic `fruits`. The `fruits-processor` `CamelSource` applies the Content Based Router EIP to process the data. The following listing describes the `fruits-processor` `CamelSource`:

```
apiVersion: sources.eventing.knative.dev/v1alpha1
kind: CamelSource
metadata:
  name: fruits-processor
spec:
  source:
    integration:
      dependencies:
        - camel:log
        - camel:kafka
        - camel:jackson
```

```
          - camel:bean
      flow:
        from:
          uri: "kafka:fruits?brokers=my-cluster-kafka-bootstrap.kafka:9092" ❶
          steps:
            - log:
                message: "Received Body ${body}"
            - unmarshal:
                json: {} ❷
            - choice: ❸
                when:
                  - simple: "${body[nutritions][sugar]} <= 5"
                    steps:
                      - remove-headers: "*"
                      - marshal:
                          json: {}
                      - set-header: ❹
                          name: ce-type
                          constant: low-sugar
                      - set-header:
                          name: fruit-sugar-level
                          constant: low
                      - to: "log:low?showAll=true&multiline=true"
                  - simple: "${body[nutritions][sugar]} > 5 || \
                              ${body[nutritions][sugar]} <= 10"
                    steps:
                      - remove-headers: "*"
                      - marshal:
                          json: {}
                      - set-header:
                          name: ce-type
                          constant: medium-sugar
                      - set-header:
                          name: fruit-sugar-level
                          constant: medium
                      - to: "log:medium?showAll=true&multiline=true"
                otherwise:
                  steps:
                    - remove-headers: "*"
                    - marshal:
                        json: {}
                    - set-header:
                        name: ce-type
                        constant: high-sugar
                    - set-header:
                        name: fruit-sugar-level
                        constant: high
                    - to: "log:high?showAll=true&multiline=true"
      sink: ❺
        ref:
          apiVersion: eventing.knative.dev/v1alpha1
```

```
    kind: Broker
    name: default
```

❶ The Camel route connects to the Apache Kakfa Broker and the topic `fruits`.

❷ Once the data is received, it is transformed into a JSON payload.

❸ The Content Based Router pattern is using the Choice EIP. In the data processing you classify the fruits as low (sugar <= 5), medium (sugar between 5 and 10), and high (sugar > 10) based on the sugar level present in their nutrition data.

❹ Based on the data classification you will be setting the CloudEvents (*https://clou devents.io*) `type` header to be `low-sugar`, `medium-sugar`, and `high-sugar`. This header is used as one of the filter attributes in the Knative Eventing Trigger.

❺ The last step is to send the processed data to the Knative Eventing Broker named `default`:

```
$ kubectl apply -n chapter-6 -f eip/fruits-processor.yaml
```

Discussion

As the Camel-K controller takes a few minutes to deploy the `CamelSource`, you can watch the pods of the `chapter-6` namespace for its status:

```
$ watch kubectl -n chapter-6 get pods --field-selector=status.phase=Running
NAME                                      READY   STATUS    AGE
camel-k-operator-5d74595cdf-4v9qz         1/1     Running   4h17m
default-broker-filter-c6654bccf-zkw7s     1/1     Running   18m
default-broker-ingress-857698bc5b-r4zmf   1/1     Running   18m
fruits-processor-h45f7-6fdfd74cf9-nmfkn   1/1     Running   29s

$ watch kubectl get  -n chapter-6 camelsources
NAME              READY   REASON   AGE
fruits-processor  True             2m22s
```

6.11 Deploying an Event Subscriber

Problem

You want to have a web application that can display the processed data.

Solution

In this recipe we will deploy a reactive (*https://oreil.ly/9Uj09*) web application called `fruit-events-display`. It is a Quarkus (*https://quarkus.io*) Java application that will update the UI (reactively) as and when it receives the processed data from the Knative Eventing backend.

You can deploy the `fruit-events-display` application using the command:

```
$ kubectl apply -n chapter-6 \
  -f $BOOK_HOME/install/utils/fruit-events-display.yaml
```

Verify if the `fruit-events-display` application is up and running:

```
$ watch kubectl -n chapter-6 get pods --field-selector=status.phase=Running
NAME                                       READY   STATUS    AGE
camel-k-operator-5d74595cdf-4v9qz          1/1     Running   4h21m
default-broker-filter-c6654bccf-zkw7s      1/1     Running   22m
default-broker-ingress-857698bc5b-r4zmf    1/1     Running   22m
fruit-events-display-8d47bc98f-6r7zt       1/1     Running   15s
fruits-processor-h45f7-6fdfd74cf9-nmfkn    1/1     Running   4m12s
```

Discussion

Because the web application will refresh its UI as and when it receives the processed data, you need you open the web application in your browser. Run the following command to open the `fruit-events-display` web application in your browser as shown in Figure 6-2:

```
$ minikube -n chapter-6 service fruit-events-display
```

Figure 6-2. Fruit-events-display web application

Figure 6-2 depicts the `fruit-events-display` application with an empty list because there is one more step. The next recipe will explain how to make the `fruit-events-display` refresh itself by reacting to the data processed by `fruits-processor`.

6.12 Filtering Data with Knative Eventing

Problem

You may want to filter the Knative Eventing data before dispatching it to the Subscriber.

Solution

In this recipe you will deploy a Knative Event Trigger called `fruits-trigger`. The Trigger consumes the events from the Knative Event Broker named `default`, and when the fruit event is received it will dispatch the events to the Subscriber—that is, `fruit-events-display` service:

```
apiVersion: eventing.knative.dev/v1alpha1
kind: Trigger
metadata:
  name: sugary-fruits
spec:
  broker: default ❶
  filter: ❷
    attributes:
      type: low-sugar
  subscriber: ❸
    ref:
      apiVersion: v1
      kind: Service
      name: fruit-events-display
```

❶ The Knative Event Broker that this Trigger listens to for Knative events. Events originate from the `CamelSource` called `fruits-processor` and are sent to the Knative Eventing Broker named `default`.

❷ The `filter` attribute restricts the events that `fruit-events-display` will receive. In this example, it is configured to filter the events for the type `low-sugar`. You could also use the other classifications of fruits such as `medium-sugar` or `high-sugar`.

❸ Set the `subscriber` as the `fruit-events-display` Kubernetes service to receive the filtered event data.

You can deploy the Knative Event Trigger using the following command:

```
$ kubectl apply -n chapter-6 -f eip/sugary-fruits.yaml
```

Discussion

You can check the status of the Trigger using the command `kubectl -n chapter-6 get triggers`, which should return one Trigger called `sugary-fruits` with a ready state as shown in the following code. As the Trigger will dispatch its filtered event to `fruit-events-display`, the Subscriber URI of the Trigger will be that of `fruit-events-display` service:

```
$ kubectl -n chapter-6 get triggers
NAME            READY BROKER
sugary-fruits   True  default
SUBSCRIBER_URI
http://fruits-events-display.chapter-6.svc.cluster.local/
```

Now you have all the needed components to check the end-to-end flow of the streaming data pipeline. To verify the data flow and processing, call the `fruits-producer` service using the script *$BOOK_HOME/bin/call.sh* with the parameters `fruits-producer` and ":

```
$ $BOOK_HOME/bin/call.sh fruits-producer ''
```

Assuming everything worked well, you should see the `low-sugar` fruits listed in the `fruits-event-display` as shown in Figure 6-3.

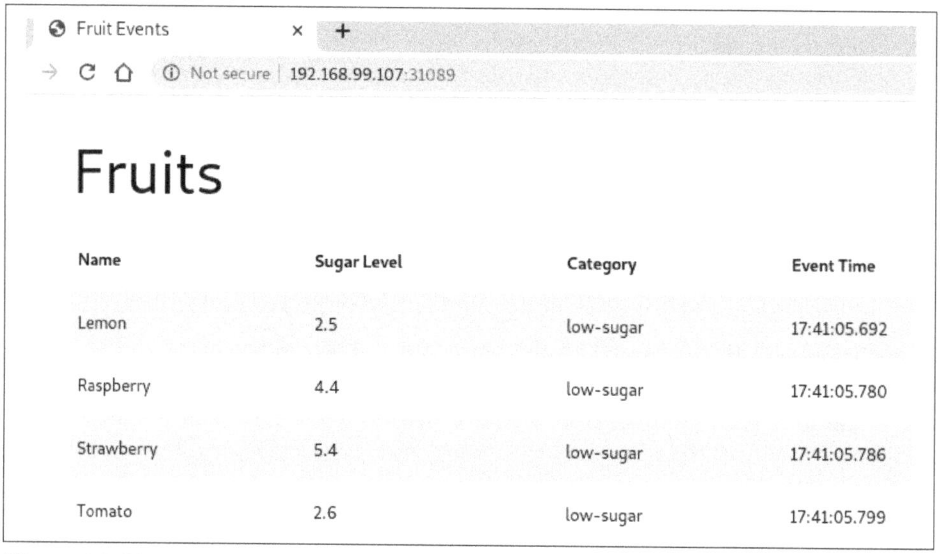

Figure 6-3. Fruit events

Now that you have a basic understanding of Apache Camel-K and how to use it to build serverless integrations, we recommend that you visit the Apache Camel (*https://oreil.ly/vaLkg*) and Apache Camel-K (*https://oreil.ly/iX9EQ*) project repositories to explore more examples.

CHAPTER 7

Knative on OpenShift

OpenShift (*https://openshift.com*) is Red Hat's distribution of Kubernetes for building and hosting enterprise-grade cloud native applications. OpenShift enables enterprises to embark upon their hybrid cloud journey by providing a unified developer experience as well as a comprehensive and rich operator experience irrespective of the underlying cloud platform. At its core, OpenShift itself is implemented as a series of Kubernetes Custom Resource Definitions (CRDs) and Operators.

Kubernetes *Operators* (*https://oreil.ly/xMFrb*) are software extensions that allow you to manage the deployment of Kubernetes applications and services. Operators not only provide automated installation, but can also manage the complete lifecycle of the software including upgrades and monitoring. Operators themselves are managed by the Operator Lifecycle Manager (*https://oreil.ly/rXBqG*).

OperatorHub.io (*https://operatorhub.io*) provides a place to share and discover Operators that have been contributed by the Kubernetes community, such as Apache Kafka (*https://oreil.ly/EIc6c*), Redis (*https://oreil.ly/Evcko*), Jenkins (*https://oreil.ly/C7ORZ*), and many others.

This chapter is aimed at OpenShift developers who want to build and deploy serverless applications on OpenShift. The recipes in this chapter will help these developers get Knative installed and configured on OpenShift using the Operators. You will see that Knative service deployment is going to be similar to what you did with vanilla Kubernetes.

7.1 Installing Knative Serving

Problem

You want to install Knative Serving on OpenShift.

Solution

Knative support for OpenShift (aka OpenShift Serverless) is available only from OpenShift v4. To install Knative on OpenShift, you will need to have an OpenShift v4 cluster and a user with cluster administrative privileges.

The fastest way to have your own OpenShift cluster is to choose your infrastructure provider from try.openshift.com (*https://try.openshift.com*) as shown in Figure 7-1 and follow the on-screen instructions to get your OpenShift cluster provisioned in less than thirty minutes.

You can install Knative Serving on OpenShift using the OpenShift Serverless Operator.

 The creation of the OpenShift cluster itself is beyond the scope of this book; however, if you are new to OpenShift, make sure to review the relevant documentation, especially the points related to how to configure your AWS (*https://oreil.ly/zHEn6*), Azure (*https://oreil.ly/BsZ1z*), or GCP (*https://oreil.ly/ZIs7L*) account. You can create a free Red Hat Developer (*https://developers.redhat.com/register*) account to access *try.openshift.com*, and once your AWS/Azure/GCP account is correctly configured, cluster creation is simply a matter of answering a few questions:

```
openshift-install --dir=myawscluster create cluster
? SSH Public Key /Users/developer/.ssh/ocp4aws.pub
? Platform aws
? Region eu-west-1
? Base Domain myroute53domain.com
? Cluster Name aws
? Pull Secret [? for help] *******
```

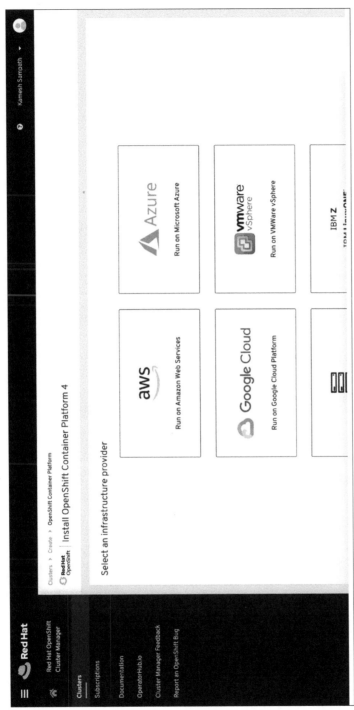

Figure 7-1. The OpenShift (https://try.openshift.com) installation page (large format version (https://oreil.ly/knative-cookbook-figs))

Discussion

Once you have your cluster ready, you also need to download the latest OpenShift client (oc). oc is analogous to kubectl, and it allows you to interact and perform various operations on an OpenShift cluster. You can download oc from the OpenShift public mirror (*https://oreil.ly/DuOOq*), unzip it, and add it to your *$PATH*. You can then verify the oc version using the command oc version as shown in the following snippet:

```
$ oc version
Client Version: v4.4.0
Server Version: 4.2.10
Kubernetes Version: v1.14.6+17b1cc6
```

> At the time of writing, the versions listed here were the latest for the OpenShift client and server versions. You can use 4.2 or above for the recipes in this chapter.

The OpenShift Administrator Console has the OperatorHub integrated (Figure 7-2) directly into it out-of-the-box. This user interface (UI) enables you to install the software infrastructure that you require without leaving the browser and with just few button clicks.

You can install Knative Serving and Eventing on OpenShift using their respective Operators from the OperatorHub. There are two ways to get the Knative Operators installed:

- Using the OperatorHub UI via the OpenShift Administrator Console
- Using the oc command-line tool, as Operators are nothing but sets of Kubernetes manifests that can be installed using oc apply -f *<your manifest file>*

For the recipes in this chapter you will be using the UI-based approach. If you are interested in the CLI–based approach, check out the Knative Tutorial (*https://bit.ly/knative-tutorial*), which has the instructions to install the Operators using the oc tool.

The OpenShift Serverless Operator (aka Knative Serving component) installs an Istio ingress gateway and Istio pilot in a namespace called knative-serving-ingress, before installing the Knative Serving core components:

1. Select the OpenShift Serverless Operator from the OperatorHub (Figure 7-3).

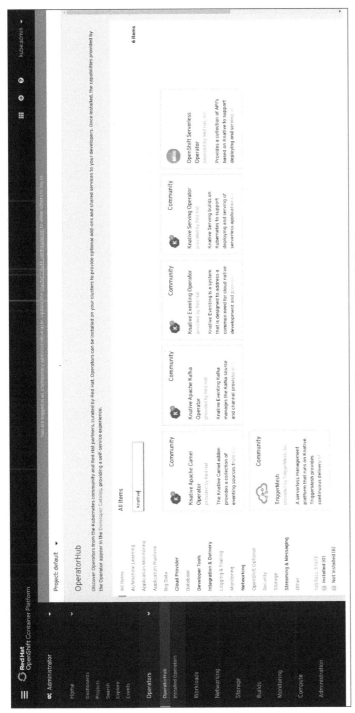

Figure 7-2. OperatorHub (large format version (https://oreil.ly/knative-cookbook-figs))

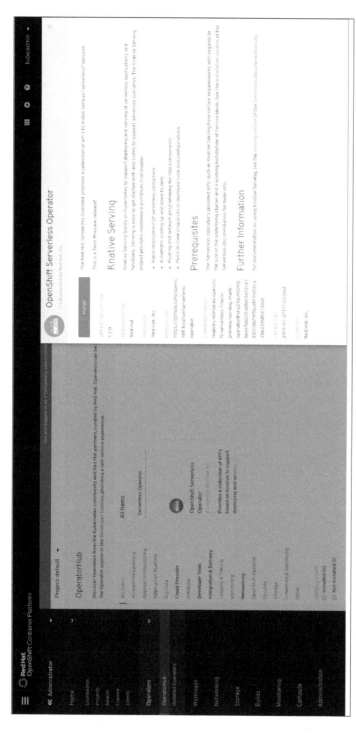

Figure 7-3. Selecting OpenShift Serverless Operator (large format version (https://oreil.ly/knative-cookbook-figs))

2. Click the Install button to start the Knative Serving installation onto the Open-Shift cluster.

3. Leaving all the options with default values as shown in Figure 7-4, click the Subscribe button.

It will take a few minutes for the Operator to be available. A successful install is shown in Figure 7-5.

You can monitor the progress of the Operator installations using the `watch` command, looking for Succeeded with the following command (modified to fit within the printed page-width requirements):

```
$ watch oc get csv
NAME                           DISPLAY                        VERSION  PHASE
elasticsearch-operator.4.2     Elasticsearch Operator         4.2      Succeeded
jaeger-operator.v1.13.1        Jaeger Operator                1.13.1   Succeeded
kiali-operator.v1.0.9          Kiali Operator                 1.0.9    Succeeded
serverless-operator.v1.3.0     OpenShift Serverless Operator  1.3.0    Succeeded
servicemeshoperator.v1.0.4     Red Hat OpenShift Service Mesh 1.0.4    Succeeded
```

The Serverless Operator (`serverless-operator`) installs not only itself but also its dependencies. In this case, Knative has a dependency on Istio (`servicemesh operator`) and Istio has a dependency on the Jaeger, Kiali, and Elasticsearch operators.

Now that you have the Serverless Operator installed, you still need to install Knative Serving itself. Create a new project called `knative-serving` as shown in Figure 7-6.

The installation of the OpenShift Serverless Operator in all namespaces (which is the default and recommended option) will cause the Operator to be copied into the `knative-serving` namespace (Figure 7-7) automatically. Wait a few minutes as this process may take some time.

 Wait for the Operators to be copied before proceeding to the next steps.

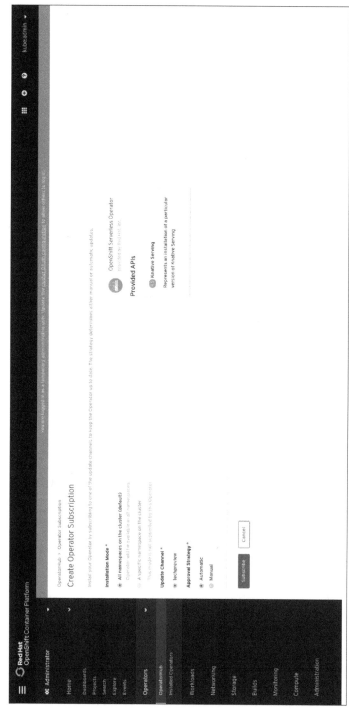

Figure 7-4. Install Serverless Operator (large format version (https://oreil.ly/knative-cookbook-figs))

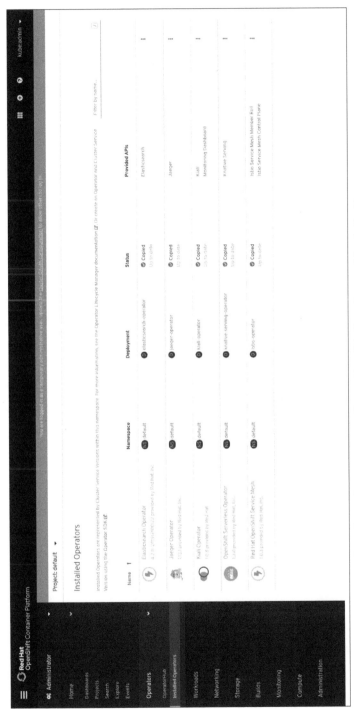

Figure 7-5. Operators installing (large format version (https://oreil.ly/knative-cookbook-figs))

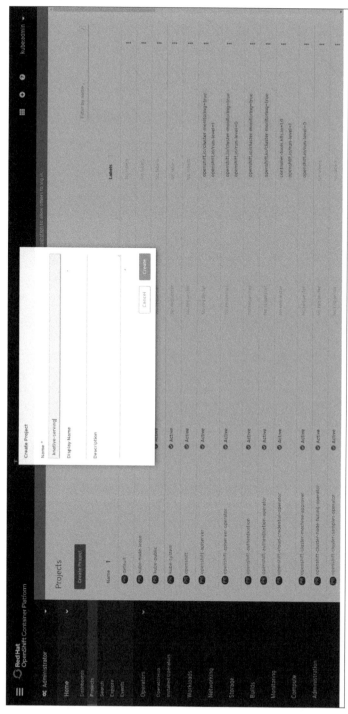

Figure 7-6. Knative Serving project (large_format version (https://oreil.ly/knative-cookbook-figs))

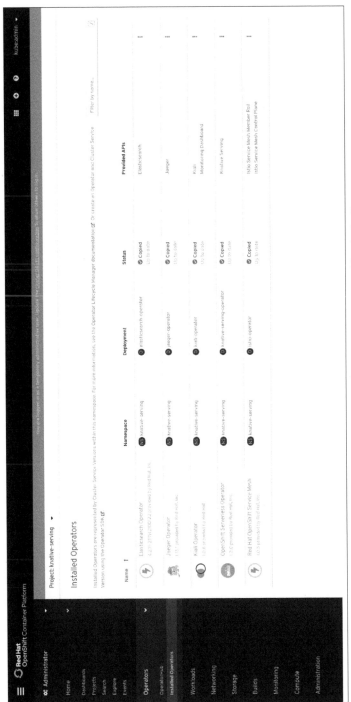

Figure 7-7. Operators copying (large format version (https://oreil.ly/knative-cookbook-figs))

Click the `Knative Serving` hyperlink from the Provided APIs column as shown in Figure 7-7.

Click the Create Knative Serving button as shown in Figure 7-8, take the default settings, and click Create as shown in Figure 7-9 to start the installation of the Knative Serving components.

It will take a few minutes for the installation to complete. You can watch the status of the pods on the namespace `knative-serving` with the following command:

```
$ watch oc get pods -n knative-serving
NAME                              READY   STATUS    AGE
activator-947bd7448-j6r6d         1/1     Running   2m52s
autoscaler-57668c89b7-hsnlm       1/1     Running   2m51s
autoscaler-hpa-9bf98ff7b-jhs6b    1/1     Running   2m52s
controller-649c9f8d97-j9966       1/1     Running   2m47s
networking-istio-6fdb7457fd-mdwpw 1/1     Running   2m44s
webhook-85484bbfc4-bqpl8          1/1     Running   2m46s
```

 You can also view the list of pods from the Workloads → Pods menu in the OpenShift Administrator Console.

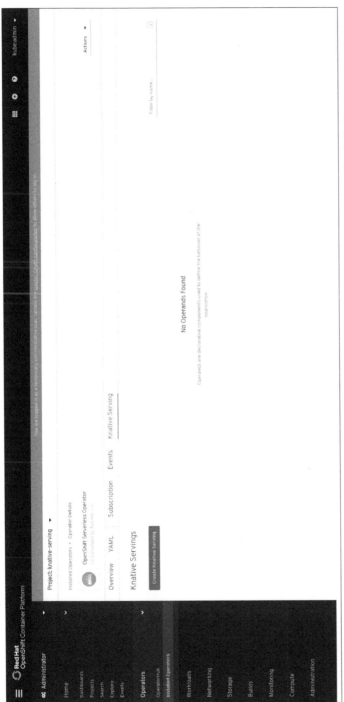

Figure 7-8. Create Knative Serving subscription (large format version (https://oreil.ly/knative-cookbook-figs))

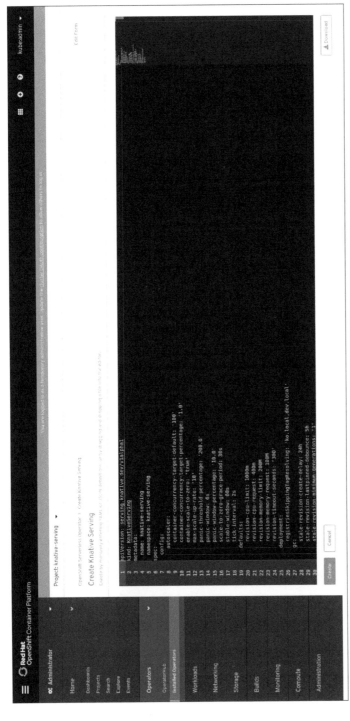

Figure 7-9. Deploy Knative Serving (large format version (https://oreil.ly/knative-cookbook-figs))

7.2 Deploying a Knative Service

Problem

You want to deploy a Knative Service on OpenShift.

Solution

There are two ways to deploy a Knative Service on OpenShift:

- The same method as a vanilla Kubernetes cluster using `oc apply -f service.yaml`
- The Developer Console method

Discussion

You can deploy Knative Service in OpenShift using one of the two methods:

- CLI method
- Developer Console method

CLI method

Deploy the same `greeter` service that has been used in the earlier chapters of this cookbook with the following steps:

1. Create a new OpenShift project called `chapter-7`:
   ```
   $ oc new-project chapter-7
   ```
2. Navigate to the *$BOOK_HOME/basics* directory and run the following command:
   ```
   $ oc apply -n chapter-7 -f service.yaml
   ```

The first deployment of the service will take some time as the container images need to be downloaded to your cluster. You can check the status of pods in the `chapter-7` namespace:

```
$ watch oc -n chapter-7 get pods
NAME                                    READY   STATUS
greeter-v1-deployment-5749cc98fc-gs6zr  2/2     Running
```

 This is a Knative Serving Service and it might have disappeared while you were busy elsewhere as it was automatically scaled-to-zero. You can also use `watch oc get ksvc` to monitor the deployment status of `greeter`.

Developer console method

The Developer Console method is behind +Add menu item as shown in Figure 7-10.
Select the Container Image option.

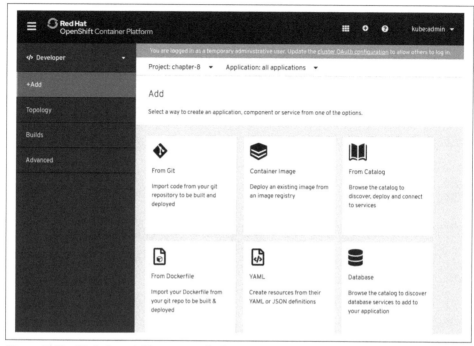

Figure 7-10. Click the +Add menu and select Container Image

Enter the name of a container image that is known to deploy well on OpenShift, such as `openshift/hello-openshift`, and click the magnifying glass icon as shown in Figure 7-11.

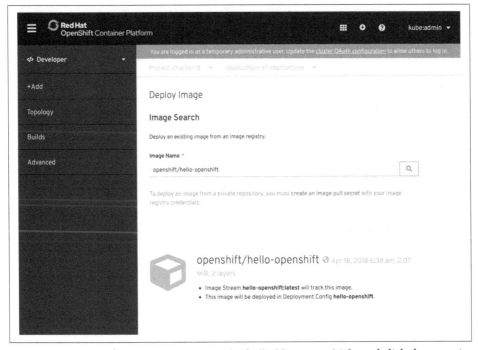

Figure 7-11. Enter the Image Name `openshift/hello-openshift` and click the magnifying glass

Scroll down the screen until you see "Enable scaling to zero when idle," and check the box as shown in Figure 7-12.

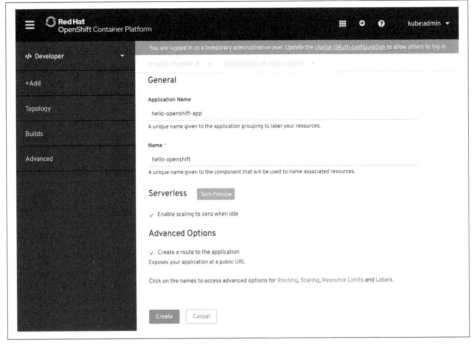

Figure 7-12. Enable scaling to zero when idle

Also make sure to check the checkbox for "Create a route to the application" and then click the Create button. Wait a few moments for the container image to be downloaded into your cluster, and your Knative service will come to life and be visible inside the OpenShift Developer Console's Topology view, as shown in Figure 7-13.

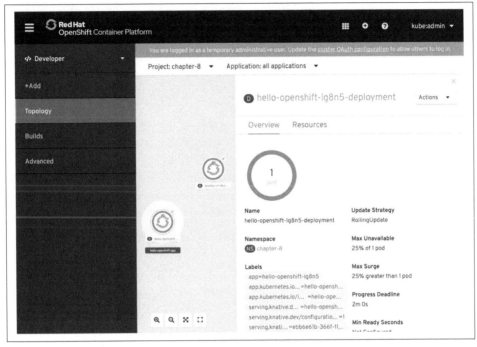

Figure 7-13. Topology view

7.3 Verifying and Invoking a Knative Service

Problem

You want to check and invoke the Knative Service's route once it becomes available.

Solution

You need to watch for the Knative route's readiness state using the oc command.

Discussion

Each Knative route creates a Knative ingress, which might not be ready immediately after the service is deployed.

When the service is deployed, the command `oc -n chapter-7 get rt greeter` will return a response as shown in following listing. `IngressNotConfigured` under REASON means the Knative ingress for the route is still being created and configured.

```
$ watch oc -n chapter-7 get rt
NAME        URL                                                      READY
greeter     http://greeter.knativetutorial.apps.azr.workspace7.org   Unknown
REASON
IngressNotConfigured
```

Wait until the route READY status is `True` before using the route in your service calls:

```
$ oc -n chapter-7 rt
NAME        URL                                                      READY
greeter     http://greeter.knativetutorial.apps.azr.workspace7.org   True
REASON
```

You can now invoke the service using the route URL http://greeter.knativetuto rial.apps.azr.workspace7.org either in your browser or from the CLI using `curl`. A successful invocation will have response like `Hi greeter => '9861675f8845' : 1` as seen in the following:

```
$ curl http://greeter.knativetutorial.apps.azr.workspace7.org
Hi  greeter => 9861675f8845 : 1
```

If you receive the message `Application is not available`, that is an indicator that your Knative Serving Service did not deploy successfully. To learn more, use the following command:

```
$ oc get ksvc
NAME        URL                                                      READY
greeter     http://greeter.knativetutorial.apps.azr.workspace7.org   False
REASON
RevisionMissing
```

`RevisionMissing` could mean that the pod was unable to schedule within the cluster. Check the cluster events stream with the following command and look for the telltale sign of `FailedScheduling`:

```
$ *oc get events --sort-by=.metadata.creationTimestamp*
...
8m8s        Warning   FailedScheduling      pod/greeter-v1-deployment-5db4d86bc-
rxw8l       0/6 nodes are available: 3 Insufficient cpu, 3 node(s) had taints that
the pod didn't tolerate.
```

The default worker node size via `try.openshift.com` on AWS in particular is very small. The quick solution is to simply increase your worker node pool via the Open-Shift Administrator Console.

The Administrator → Compute → Machine Sets option in the OpenShift Administrator Console will allow you to simply point and click to add a new worker node. This process can take a few minutes, but once the node joins the cluster you can then delete and re-add the Knative Service.

Other possible deployment issues might simply be a container image that is not downloadable to your cluster, and `oc get events` is very helpful in terms of debugging various situations.

You have successfully installed Knative Serving in OpenShift, deployed your first Knative Service, and called that service. You can continue your learning journey by attempting other recipes from this cookbook with your OpenShift cluster.

Index

CloudEvent SDK, 48
CloudEvents (CE)
    about, 43, 44, 47
    displaying messages, 104
    logging messages, 104
cold start latency, 39-42
concurrency metric, 33
config-observability, 72
ConfigMap, 6, 34, 72
configuring
    Apache Camel-K for speed, 95
    Channels, 58
    container registry aliases, 6-8
    Knative Service to handle request spikes,
       37-39
    Knative Services for autoscaling, 34
connecting sources to services, 49
container environment, verifying, 13-15
container registry aliases, configuring, 6-8
ContainerSource, 46
Content Based Router, 107
Contour gateway, 8
contribution repository, 103
controller infrastructure component, 11
cpu metric, 33
CPUS environment variable, 4
CRDs (Custom Resource Definitions), 9, 10,
    102, 117
CronJobSource, 46, 49
curl command, 23, 66
custom columns file, 75
Custom Resource Definitions (CRDs), 9, 10,
    102, 117
customer service, 74
customizing kubectl output columns, 75

D

daemonset, 6
dashboards
    autoscale debugging, 78
    Grafana, 77
    Knative Serving - Revision HTTP Requests,
       85
data filtering, with Knative Eventing, 114
data processor, 108, 111-113
data producer, 108, 109-111
deploying
    Apache Kafka cluster, 50-53
    data processor, 111-113

data producer, 109-111
event subscribers, 113
Grafana, 70-71
Knative Eventing Service, 47-49
Knative Service, 131-135
Knative Serving, 19-23
observable test services, 74
Prometheus, 70-71
Sonatype Nexus, 96
Developer Console method, 131
displaying CloudEvents (CE) messages, 104
distributing traffic between Knative Service
    revisions, 26
docker tool, 1
Domain Specific Language (DSL), 93
Durability, as feature of messaging-based archi-
    tecture, 58

E

enabling Prometheus for metrics collection, 72
Enterprise Integration Patterns (EIP), 93,
    107-109
Event Subscriber (Fruits UI), 108
event trigger, 108
events
    Apache Kafka, 53-56
    deploying subscribers, 113
    producing with eventing sources, 45
    receiving with Knative Eventing Sinks, 46

F

filter attribute, 115
filters, 68, 114-116
Function as a Service (FaaS), 1

G

GCP account, 118
GCP PubSub, 44, 58
git tool, 1
Gloo gateway, 8
Grafana
    about, 69
    dashboards, 77
    deploying, 70-71
greeter serice, 23

H

helm tool, 1, 3

querying Kubernetes resources, 14-15

R

Reactive web application, 113
readiness probe, 21
recommendation service, 74
Red Hat Developer account, 118
Redis, 117
request spikes, configuring Knative Service to handle, 37-39
Request Volume panel (Knative Serving - Revision HTTP Requests dashboard), 85
requests per second metric, 33
Resource Usage panel (autoscale debugging dashboard), 78
Response Volume panel (Knative Serving - Revision HTTP Requests dashboard), 85
restricting Knative Service visibility, 76-81
revision, 23
Revision Pod Counts panel (autoscale debugging dashboard), 78
revisionName attribute, 27
revisions, distributing traffic between Knative Service, 26
running Apache Camel-K integrations as Knative serverless services, 100-103

S

scale-to-zero, 33, 35
scale-to-zero-grace-period, 35
Server-Sent Events (SSE), 107
serverless integration patterns, 93-116
    about, 93
    applying Enterprise Integration Patterns with Apache Camel-K, 107-109
    configuring Apache Camel-K for speed, 95
    deploying data processor, 111-113
    deploying data producer, 109-111
    deploying event subscribers, 113
    displaying CloudEvents (CE) messages, 104
    filtering data with Knative Eventing, 114-116
    installing Apache Camel-K, 94
    logging CloudEvents (CE) messages, 104
    running Apache Camel-K integrations as Knative serverless services, 100-103
    using Apache Camel-K, 93-116
    using Knative Eventing with Apache Camel-K, 103

wiring CamelSource to Knative Eventing Sink, 104-107
writing Apache Camel-K integration, 96-100
Serverless Operator, 123
serverless-style architecture, 33
service-pinned.yaml, 29
Sieve of Eratosthenes, 38
SinkBindings, 46
sleep parameter, 39
Sonatype Nexus, 95
Source to Sink, 43
sourcing Apache Kafka events with Knative Eventing, 53-56
spec block, 20
SSE (Server-Sent Events), 107
stable-window, 35
stern tool, 1, 3
Strimzi, 50
subscriptions, 44, 59-63
switching namespaces, 13

T

tag attribute, 27
termination period, 36
tools, installing required, 1-4
tracing Knative Services with Jaeger, 88-92
traffic, distributing between Knative Service revisions, 26
Triggers
    about, 44
    event trigger, 108
    using, 63-68
twelve-factor app, 19

U

updating Knative Service configurations, 23-26
upto parameter, 39
usage patterns, 43-45

V

verifying
    container environment, 13-15
    Knative Service, 135
ver_knas, 137
VM_DRIVER environment variable, 4

W

watch command, 14, 36
watch tool, 1, 3
webhook infrastructure component, 11
wiring CamelSource to Knative Eventing Sink, 104-107
writing Apache Camel-K integration, 96-100

X

x-b3 headers, 73

Y

YAML resources, 19
yq v2.4.1 tool, 1, 3

About the Authors

Burr Sutter (@burrsutter) is a lifelong developer advocate, community organizer, technology evangelist, and featured speaker at technology events around the globe—from Bangalore to Brussels and Berlin to Beijing (and most parts in between). He is currently Red Hat's Director of Developer Experience. A Java Champion since 2005 and former president of the Atlanta Java User Group, Burr founded the DevNexus conference, now the second-largest Java event in the United States. When spending time away from the computer, he enjoys going off-grid in the jungles of Mexico and the bush of Kenya. You can find Burr online at *burrsutter.com*.

Kamesh Sampath (@kamesh_sampath) is a Principal Software Engineer at Red Hat. As part of his additional role as Director of Developer Experience at Red Hat and a Google Developer Expert, he actively educates on Java, Kubernetes/OpenShift, Servicemesh, and Serverless technologies. With a career spanning close to two decades, most of Kamesh's career was with the services industry helping various enterprise customers build Java-based solutions. Kamesh has been a contributor to open source projects for more than a decade, and he now actively contributes to projects like Knative, Camel-K, Quarkus, Eclipse Che, etc. As part of his developer philosophy he strongly believes in LEARN MORE, DO MORE, and SHARE MORE! You can connect with Kamesh on GitHub at *github.com/kameshsampath* or LinkedIn at *linkedin.com/in/kameshsampath*, and can find his blog at *developers.redhat.com*.

Colophon

The animal on the cover of *Knative Cookbook* is a Steller's eider duck (*Polysticta stelleri*). This species of sea duck is native to the Arctic, breeding and nesting in northern Alaska, Russia, and Siberia, and spending winters in the Alaskan peninsula and the Aleutian Islands. The Steller's eider is also called *Igniquaqtuq* or "the bird that sat in fire" by the Iñupiat people due to the "burnt" coloring of the male's belly.

The Steller's eider duck is the smallest of the eiders, and are more agile than the others both in flight and on land. They can grow up to 18 inches and have a large head with a long bill and tail. Males are typically more colorful, with a distinctive white head and shoulder patches, tan and deep brown shading on the underbelly, black eye spots, and a blue-black collar around the neck that extends down the back and tail. Females are mostly deep brown, but both have iridescent blue wing patches edged in white. While at sea, the Steller's eider feeds on mollusks, crustaceans, echinoderms, and small fish; on the tundra they eat a number of aquatic insects, as well as grasses, sedges, and pondweed.

These ducks travel in flocks for most of the year, migrating side by side a few feet above the water along the coast. They migrate north to breed beginning in late April and reach their nesting sites by early June. Females will remain on the breeding grounds until the new chicks are able to fly, but the males will leave in early July to molt. Steller's eiders are solitary breeders that pair-bond during the winter. They court in groups of up to seven males per single female, performing courtship displays and showing aggression to one another. Females build nests and incubate their eggs alone.

The Steller's eider is categorized as a vulnerable species by the International Union for Conservation of Nature. Threats to the duck include natural predators such as foxes and snowy owls, as well as lead poisoning, contaminants, and changes in the marine environment over time. Many of the animals on O'Reilly covers are endangered; all of them are important to the world.

The cover illustration is by Karen Montgomery, based on a black and white engraving from *British Birds*. The cover fonts are Gilroy Semibold and Guardian Sans. The text font is Adobe Minion Pro; the heading font is Adobe Myriad Condensed; and the code font is Dalton Maag's Ubuntu Mono.

O'REILLY®

There's much more where this came from.

Experience books, videos, live online training courses, and more from O'Reilly and our 200+ partners—all in one place.

Learn more at oreilly.com/online-learning

©2019 O'Reilly Media, Inc. O'Reilly is a registered trademark of O'Reilly Media, Inc. | 175

Milton Keynes UK
Ingram Content Group UK Ltd.
UKHW050105211223
434727UK00004B/16

9 781492 061199